"I Loved My Mother on Saturdays" and other tales from the shtetl and beyond

by Roslyn Bresnick-Perry

Edited & with an introduction
by Caren Schnur Neile

Published by Ben Yehuda Press
430 Kensington Road
Teaneck, NJ 07666

http://www.BenYehudaPress.com

Ben Yehuda Press books may be purchased for educational, business or sales promotional use.
For information, please contact:
Special Markets, Ben Yehuda Press,
430 Kensington Road, Teaneck, NJ 07666.
markets@BenYehudaPress.com.

pb ISBN 1-934730-30-0
pb ISBN13 978-1-934730-30-0

Library of Congress Cataloging-in-Publication Data

Bresnick-Perry, Roslyn.
I loved my mother on Saturdays and other tales from the shtetl and beyond / by Roslyn Bresnick-Perry ; edited & with an introduction by Caren Schnur Neile.
p. cm.
ISBN 978-1-934730-30-0
1. Bresnick-Perry, Roslyn. 2. Memorates. 3. Jews--Belarus. 4. Jews--United States. 5. Jews--Social life and customs. I. Neile, Caren S. II. Title.

GR98.B68 2009
305.892'4073--dc22

2009000002

As you are at seven, so you are at seventy.
-Jewish proverb

I am from a lost world of blood-soaked earth.
I am from the sounds of words searching for ears.
I am from tears lost in the babble of strange landscapes.
I am from immigrants who cannot please their Irish teacher because she hates Yiddish accents.
I am from blind leaders.
Elders who have lost the old
and have not yet found the new.
I am from dirty streets and clean houses.
I am from cries emanating from throats made dumb by toil and despair.
I am from neighbors sitting outside on wooden folding chairs, cracking sunflower seeds and telling stories.
I am from spring, birthing roots into the weed-choked cracks of sidewalks.
I am from rebels wanting to change the world.
I am a sponge for knowing.
I am my own beginning.
-Roslyn Bresnick-Perry

Contents

A New World

Acknowledgments

First and foremost I want to thank Caren Neile, my editor, mentor and dear friend without whose inspiration and encouragement these stories would never have evolved into a book. I also want to thank my fellow storytellers, friends, and family who had to hear these stories many times before they were performed. I have benefited enormously from their responses and suggestions. I wish I could express my thanks to all the people of my stories, but since the people of my childhood were brutally murdered during the Holocaust, my hope is that they will be remembered through my short and loving involvement with them. However, I thank all the others who were and are part of my life and who gave life to my stories.

Roslyn

A note on Hebrew & Yiddish spelling

In transliterating Hebrew and Yiddish expressions, I have generally followed the "Litvak" pronunciation I grew up with. Appropriately enough, this pronuncation turned "oh"s into "oy"s. Thus, "Toyre," not "Torah."

Introduction

Roslyn Bresnick-Perry and the Personal Politics of Storytelling

by Caren Schnur Neile, MFA, Ph.D.

> Oh my, did I love sauerkraut! In fact, I told my grandfather that I loved sauerkraut even better than I loved my favorite cousin Yossele, who I would someday marry.
>
> —"Succos is for Sauerkraut"

I put off meeting Roslyn Bresnick-Perry for years. We had several friends and colleagues in common among professional storytellers, and my home is not ten minutes from her winter residence in a Florida senior citizen community. I had even quoted her as saying, "You can't hate someone once you hear his story" countless times in class and in print. Again and again I was told, "Oh, you must meet Roslyn! You're going to love her!"

Now, as anybody who knows the American storytelling community will tell you, there is a lot of love floating around. In fact, some say too much. After presenting a workshop at the annual conference of our professional organization, the National Storytelling Network, the celebrated scholar of fairy tales Jack Zipes published an article in the national press about how oddly "nice" we are. It has even been suggested that this niceness could be a problem for the current revival of adult performance storytelling, preventing many tellers from branching out into mass culture and from engaging in constructive criticism both of our movement and of our work.

So when I was told I simply must meet an eighty-year-old grandmother who told stories of the shtetl, the now-extinct ghetto in

Eastern Europe, I had no doubt that I would enjoy her company. I just felt no particular need to go out of my way to meet yet another lovely, loving storyteller. Cold, maybe. Practical? I thought so.

It was not until I hosted the great Illinois storyteller Jim May at Florida Atlantic University in 2002 that I finally met Roslyn. My first impression was of a round-faced, ruddy-cheeked woman with short white hair and smiling eyes. But then, after the concert, when Jim, Roslyn and I sat in the school cafeteria trading stories, I noticed those eyes flash with an unmistakable devilishness and the mouth turn up in a knowing smile. I suddenly recognized that this sweet-faced senior citizen was eighty going on eight. All, in other words, was not quite what it seemed—which just happens to be the essence of storytelling. And so, from that day on, I grew to love Roslyn.

* * *

To understand the work of Roslyn Bresnick-Perry, it is necessary to understand her world, both personal and professional. She was born Raizele Kolner in 1922 in Wysokie-Litewskie, in Belarus, in the former Soviet Union. Perry's roots are in a landscape of sparkling waterways flowing through lush fields and fragrant forests. Her town was a shtetl, one of hundreds of small communities in pre-World War II Europe that were comprised of religious Jews and non-Jewish, mostly agrarian, peasants. While Christian residents opposed permanent Jewish settlement in the larger cities, Polish landowners rented their towns, villages, and inns to Jews, who in turn created their small communities. In this way, the Jews maintained both their history and culture, particularly the Yiddish language, a mixture of mainly German and Hebrew, written in Hebrew characters.

With the advent of Russian rule, the Jews became the victims of virulent anti-Semitism, most notably in the form of massacres called pogroms. The violence, prohibitions against land ownership, and other restrictions led to massive Jewish immigration to the Ukraine or to southern Russia, and, from the 1880s on, to the United States.

Raizele and her mother came to Ellis Island in 1929, meeting her father, who had emigrated years earlier. They settled in the Bronx, where two more children were born. In the afternoons when public school let out, Raizele attended the school of the Workmen's Circle, or Arbeiter Ring, a Jewish-Socialist mutual aid society created by secular, radical-minded European immigrants at the end of the nineteenth century. Dyslexia channeled her talents into fashion when she could not enter the academic world. She was trained in fashion design and soon climbed the ranks of the New York garment industry. By then a wife and mother, she went on to tackle the challenge of her learning disability and entered college at age fifty-six, earning Bachelors and Masters degrees. It was during an admissions interview for a doctoral program in the mid-1980s that a Columbia University advisor suggested that rather than get a Ph.D., Roslyn should concentrate on what she did so well as a graduate student in cultural history: tell stories.

She recalls: "He asked me, 'Why do you want to spend the rest of your life in school? I know, you want to be the smartest one in the cemetery. But why don't you teach, or lecture? You have so much to give! Look, every one of your professors writes that you are a wonderful storyteller. Go out and tell stories and get paid for doing it.'"

At the time, the current American storytelling revival was in its infancy. The movement was founded largely by librarians and street performers, who in 1972 congregated in what became an annual festival. The event was spearheaded by Jimmy Neil Smith, the mayor of tiny Jonesborough (now spelled Jonesboro) in northeast Tennessee, in an effort to draw visitors to the fading Revolutionary War-era town. Emerging in the midst of a national return to American folk culture—I am thinking here of snoods, granny glasses, dulcimer playing and contra dancing—storytelling captured the imagination not only of Southerners, but of performers and audiences throughout the nation. The then-boldly named National Storytelling Festival has lived up to its name, playing host these days to 10,000 attendees over a single October weekend.

Due to her disability as much as to her cultural heritage, Roslyn well understood the power of oral narrative. Due to her background in cultural history, as well as to her extroverted nature, she knew how to connect with all sorts of people in a variety of settings. At a time when most performance tellers were infusing folktales with their own voices, Perry was one of those bringing to life her own experiences, first as a volunteer in local schools and organizations, then as a well-paid star at festivals and theaters throughout the country and abroad.

> She was not spanking me for being such a vilde khaye, a wild animal. She was not spanking me for always soiling and tearing my clothes. She was not spanking me for always being disobedient. What she was spanking me for was that her child, on whom she lavished all her time and love and affection, was going to grow up to be the world's biggest liar.
>
> –"A Can of Paint"

In our time of extraordinary technological complexity, Perry's art form can perhaps best be defined in contrast to its shadow side, that is, by what it is not. Although intensely autobiographical, it is by no means oral history. Her oeuvre contains images and archetypes: the sights, sounds and symbols of a life buffeted by history and buoyed by love and, above all, by the power of the imagination. She uses the artist's eye for observation and the entertainer's ear for the perfect punch line to sand, polish and lacquer her experiences into performance pieces that pack an emotional wallop. Neither historian nor witness, she is, rather, a professional storyteller, a purveyor of that ancient and once-revered tradition that is the forerunner to modern genealogy, history, education, and, of course, theatre. As such, she has the power to simultaneously evoke pleasure, enlightenment, inspiration and community.

Another thing Perry's work is not is a collection of short stories. Indeed, her written work is not writing as we commonly know it. In contrast to, say, Hemingway, whose literary creations were produced to be read, Perry's writing is like that of the late Spalding Gray, who published several books containing work fine-tuned over years of stage performance. This stage-to-page creative process is central to an understanding of the storyteller's art. In a culture where novelists, film directors, dancers, painters and liars are referred to as storytellers, it is essential to underscore the difference between work that is perfected at a desk in silence—and presented to the public through a visual medium—and oral performance that depends on a live audience's spontaneous reactions to be completed. Or, more correctly, it is never completed, because although Perry's book contains well-honed versions of her stories, she will never tell them exactly as they appear in these pages. That is the dynamic quality of storytelling.

The stories that constitute Perry's oeuvre are thus neither literary creations put to paper that carry the perfect pitch of literary fiction, nor are they transcriptions of past performances. Rather, we might think of them as Perry's pre-performance drafts, from which she crafts each telling.

I have arranged the stories in the form in which she wrote them, with minimal changes, to distinguish them from literary works. Depending on the situation, Roslyn's mood and her audience, she might add details, rearrange them or leave them out altogether. Because every telling thus requires a permutation of the material, there is no "definitive" version, other than that which she set on the page to refresh her memory before a gig. Each time she walks onstage, she creates a unique performance, based on what has worked in the past and how she and the audience are experiencing the present..

That is to say, as an act of "co-creation" with an audience, storytelling requires not only a framework, but also the flexibility to break from that frame. You may find here mixed tenses and, at times, the odd colloquial grammatical side-step. This is, after all, how we speak. Try to imagine, as you read these tales, a spunky, "old and bold" octogenarian—with a slight New York accent—infusing each word with her own special energy and heart. If you cannot do so, it is not due to the shortcomings of the stories, but rather to the power of the oral tradition, with its non-verbal cues that are lost to the written word.

One might well ask: If the stories presented here are not history, literature, transcription or even complete, what are they? Roslyn's work is contained in the folklore genre known as memorate, or life-experience stories. Like other forms of folk narrative, memorate is originally transmitted orally and is transformed by every teller and every telling. In our confessional age, personal memorate, the telling of one's own stories, is the fastest growing form of contemporary storytelling performance, as evidenced in part by the success of the Moth, a flourishing New York City-based enterprise that features performances of this genre in clubs, museums and other venues.

Yet despite the growth of adult performance, storytelling is still largely considered the stuff of schools, parents' laps and public library story hours. Roslyn does perform for children, and uses some of the same material she presents to adults. Like water, the story takes the shape of the vessel, or, in the case of performance, the audience. For children, she chooses difference emphases, language and descriptions.

"Children want to be entertained first and foremost," she told me recently. The story must be simple and direct, while at the same time combining action, emotion, looming failure and imminent success. It is not difficult for children to identify with the characters no matter who and what they are. Even an "it" can evoke in the child the response of "I know how that feels."

On the other hand, she says, "adult audiences appreciate human interest stories. They respond to thoughtful, comprehensive material. Although they too react to situations with 'I know how that feels,' their concern with content, form, imagination and presentation makes them much more demanding. When an adult audience rewards you with laughter and approval, when you can actually hear them breathing with you, there is no greater satisfaction in the telling of stories, especially personal ones."

One of Perry's primary areas of appeal as a storyteller is that she falls between two camps. On one hand, she is a traditional teller raised on oral storytelling by tellers with little or no formal education. Equally important, she is a modern, educated artist who knows how to craft and perform a story to maximum effect. She has the performer's charisma, that cat-that-ate-the-canary grin that tells us that the child whose stories she relates is alive and well in an adult body. In this way, she is able to capture the imagination of listeners of all ages and backgrounds. She has the storyteller's gift for bringing out the salient details that strike a universal chord.

"Take my being sideswiped by a taxicab last year," she says. "How would I shape the story? An incident happens, you think back on the ramifications of what happened. You ask yourself why it happened, how you felt when it was happening. For example, were there other people involved whose response to you and your situation helped or hindered what was going on?

"You look back on the incident not only as you experienced it, but also as an objective observer seeing what was happening. You become aware of both the dark and comic goings-on where you and the others are concerned.

"How did this incident play itself out, what did you learn, how has it impinged on your overall view of yourself and others? Has the story something to say to the people to whom you would like to tell the story? Why would you want to tell this story? Are you making some kind of statement about the culture in which you live?

"Above all, I always keep in mind that personal stories are exactly what they say—personal accounts of yours or of others you know, interacting in their daily lives within the present. They are often warm, entertaining, humorous, at times poignant, at times terribly sad, and some, downright hilarious, but they always address themselves to the 'once upon a time is now.'"

A Jewish storyteller

Throughout her illustrious career, says Perry, her primary responsibility has been to the Jewish people. She explains:

"First and foremost, I tell stories to preserve the memory of my family and the people of my town who were all destroyed in the Holocaust. To me they are not the six million Jews annihilated; to me they are my grandparents, aunts, uncles, cousins, friends among whom I spent my childhood years. I also tell personal stories to share some of the experiences of what it was like to be a Jewish immigrant child in the strange new world of America. And lastly, I tell stories of Jewish people living their lives as Americans, wrapped in their ethnicity, adding their own unique color to the mosaic that is America."

Traditionally, the Jews are avid storytellers, known both as the People of the Book and of the Spoken Word. According to tradition, the Oral Law, which was later codified into the written Talmud, was delivered to the Jews simultaneously with the Hebrew Bible, or Tanach. Aggadot, or legends, were central to this oral tradition. Thus although storytelling from sources other than the holy books was devalued, the books themselves were the basis of a rich trove of stories containing moral lessons.

Stories, both secular and otherwise, were a vital means of Jewish socialization, transmitted within families and by rabbis, teachers and professional itinerant storytellers, known as maggidim. The promotion of communitas—anthropologist Victor Turner's term for deep communal self-identification—is of paramount importance to Jewish storytelling.

> This dramatic group was originally organized to perform Bible stories like "The Selling of Joseph," or the story of Chanukah or Purim, told through satire. But it expanded its repertoire with the influx of more educated, more enlightened young actors. And I, Raizelle Kolner, was part of this troupe!
>
> —"It's Only a Purim Shpiel"

As is the case with many artists, Roslyn's perspective on her community is balanced between those of consummate insider and rebellious outsider. "Having spent my childhood in a shtetl in Eastern Europe," she says, "where so much of life was ritualized by adherence to the laws, commandments, traditions, and mythology of Jewish life, it became difficult for me to free myself from what I felt and how I saw myself as a Jew.

"I found that although I loved the rituals, symbols, ceremonies, delights of biblical study—in other words the culture—I could not accept divine authority rather then human reason. I was determined to know my people in my own way, and in turn make my observations known to others."

The decimation of the shtetl and those Jews who populated it remains, in these stories, off-screen. Raizele and her parents are safely ensconced in the Bronx, New York, when her extended family and friends are swallowed by the conflagration known as the Shoah, or Holocaust. Only in "Riding with the Moon" and "Going Home to Nowhere" do we catch the barest glimpse of the horror that befell Zisl, Bubbe, Shaine, Zayde, and the assorted aunts and uncles we meet in these pages. It is a testament to Perry's storytelling instincts and abilities that her simple, whimsical portraits of shtetl life reveal the horrors of Nazism in a way that facts and figures, maps and dates, cannot. As she says, it is not only six million people who died. Her beloved Zisl died.

* * *

The stories of Roslyn's shtetl childhood constitute the first part of this collection. In Part Two, Raizele Kolner becomes Roslyn Kollner, navigating the treacherous—especially for an immigrant child—byways of New York City. Whether it is her accent that fails her ("My First Thanksgiving"), her family ("Less Work for Mother," "The Coat"), or America ("Angelina's Garden"), she manages to emerge relatively unscathed, with a mature sense of irony and equanimity. Although Roslyn went on to excel in the academy, she demonstrates in stories like "Angelina's Garden" that her greatest life lessons were learned at home and on the streets.

> I know I made Angelina take me into her garden, but I only wanted a look," I wailed. "Then her grandmother said I was a dirty Jew and a Christ killer. I know I'm Jewish, but I know I'm not dirty, because Mama makes me wash all the time. And I know I'm not a killer. But who is Christ?
>
> —"Angelina's Garden"

At the same time that we experience the joys and defeats of the child in Perry's stories, we also confront the hardships faced by the adults in her life. Who among us would trade our lives for the plight of Roslyn's exhausted mother, who had only one day a week to feel and behave like a human being? ("I Loved My Mother on Saturdays.") Roslyn's careful enumeration of her mother's household tasks bears the skill of a reporter and the wisdom of an adult who long ago chose to forgive, if not forget.

Part Three follows Roslyn out of the Jewish ghetto and into the wider world, as demonstrated by stories such as "The Jews Are Coming! The Jews Are Coming!" Here we see her as independent fashion designer ("All in a Day's Work"), proud mother ("Fish Like Bubbe Used to Make," "Der Signal: Transmogrification of a Story"), and choosy widow ("Jack Waldman.")

We also see Roslyn, for the first time, as a storyteller.

> I recently wrote a story called "On the Subway from the Bronx" and told it to a group of women in charge of developing multicultural activities for a cooperative housing development, which not too many years earlier had been overwhelmingly Jewish. Now, there was a mix of many ethnic groups that were unaccustomed to cooperative living. The aim of the activities was to acquaint the new coop owners with the diversity of the people who lived in their midst. The women felt the story I had told them would make a perfect flyer to introduce the residents to their project. They planned to put the flyers under everyone's door.
>
> —"I'm from New Haven"

What happens when a person recognizes her role as a storyteller? Whether professional or amateur, certain features of the process are the same. Telling our stories imbues our lives with meaning, by virtue of the ethical qualities embedded in narrative. The experience of being deeply listened to, whether by friends, family, acquaintances or strangers, empowers us, causing us to acknowledge not only the value of our words, but also of our lives. Making eye contact and interacting both directly and indirectly, as oral storytelling demands, creates a deep sense of connection with others. Storytelling also promotes memory, as the sequential flow of the narrative carries us from scene to scene.

Thus reading, or better still listening to, Roslyn the storyteller not only gives us a portrait of a life, but also of the self-reflexive process of understanding and coming to terms with one's life through committing it to narrative. Yes, as professional storytellers like to say, we are all storytellers, and we process existence as a series of stories. However we do not all achieve equal success in the process. Roslyn Bresnick-Perry's stories demonstrate her evolution, through the challenge of absorbing a new language and country, the tragedy of losing the old, and the ordinary trials and rituals of growing up. In addition, they document the development of her voice, from the whispers and whimpers of a pampered child of the shtetl to the spot-on articulation of a street-wise cosmopolitan. What is more, they demonstrate the attention to language, rhythm, characterization and detail associated with a tale well-told.

* * *

> My paternal grandmother Shaine Kolner never liked me. I once asked her to name her favorite grandchildren, and she put me last on a list of seventeen. This made me feel really bad. I asked her right out, "Bubbe, why don't you like me?"
>
> She answered me just as directly: *"Vayl du bist a shtik fun dayn mame*—because you are just like your mother."
>
> — "My Grandmother Shaine Never Liked Me"

Roslyn Bresnick-Perry illuminates storytelling's past. But like most storytellers, she also has designs on the future.

"There is always a future for storytelling," she says, "just as there always was storytelling."

The need for people to tell stories is so much greater now than ever before because now we're attached by a little remote control box to the television; we don't talk to one another. There's a plethora of stories on television, but what are they saying? Television is controlled by people who want to manipulate us. There's such an urgency for storytelling; it's unbelievable.

"We must insist on this. Though storytellers are a comparatively small group, revolutions were started by small groups. We have to keep doing it, encourage more and more people to do storytelling, become active promoters.

"You know," she says, "there's nothing so sad as a heart full of stories with no one to tell them to."

You're going to love Roslyn.

The Shtetl

Succos is for Sauerkraut

My whole family loves sauerkraut. When my son was a little boy, he saw my mother make sauerkraut, just like they did in Europe, in our apartment in the Bronx. She put it in a small bowl, covered the bowl with a plate, and placed a stone on top of the plate. When my son got married and moved to California, he wanted me to give his wife his bubbe's recipe for sauerkraut, which I did.

A few days later, he called me back. "Ma," he said, "you didn't tell her what kind of stone you need."

I said, "A heavy one!" *–RBP*

Did you know that Succos is for sauerkraut? That's right, it is. It's not only for building a succah, eating in it, singing prayers in it, blessing the esrog and lulav in it. It's also a time for making sauerkraut. Ask me, because I know. We always make sauerkraut for Succos.

You see, Succos is also called the Holiday of Booths. It is the Jewish people's Thanksgiving. In olden times, in the ancient land of Judea, our ancestors built little huts in their fields when they gathered their crops in autumn. They built them of twigs and branches from trees, interlaced them with sweet-smelling myrtle and palm leaves, and hung the most perfect fruits and vegetables inside to thank God for His bounty and His love. So we had to do the same.

That's what my grandfather told me, and I knew that when my grandfather said something it was so, because that's just what we did.

Just before Succos, I go with him to gather the tall grass that grows near the pond behind the slaughterhouse. And I go with him to pick out the most perfect fruit from the peasants who bring them to the fairground on market day to hang on the walls of our succah.

And I go with him to synagogue to borrow the esrog, which is a citron, and the lulav, which is a myrtle, and palm branch to shake and bless. And I go with him to pick the vegetables from our own garden in back of the house. We not only pick sweet-tasting peas, yellow carrots and lima beans that grow on tall poles, but we also pick cabbages, lots and lots of cabbages. Not to hang on the walls, of course. The cabbages are for my grandmother, who always makes a big barrel of sauerkraut to last the whole winter.

Oh my, did I love sauerkraut! In fact, I told my grandfather that I loved sauerkraut even better than I loved my favorite cousin Yossele, who I would someday marry.

Well, this particular Succos, the Succos of our story, I go with my grandfather as I had always gone to gather the bounty for the succah. But I am growing up, and I don't want just to stand around and only watch as he and my young uncle put the succah together. I want to help. I'm big now, I'm five years old, and I also know how to hammer.

"Let me help build the succah, Zayde," I say.

My grandfather looks at me with an expression of doom.

"Please, please Zayde," I say again, in my best pleading voice. (I must tell you that my grandfather cannot refuse me anything. I am his only grandchild. My mother is his oldest daughter. His other children are younger and unmarried.)

"All right, all right," says my grandfather. "I see how big you are. All right, you can help. You can hand us the nails."

I am thrilled. That night I cannot sleep. At the crack of dawn, I run to my grandfather's house. He and my uncle Avrom Layb are already high on a ladder, building the succah. I immediately run to the nail box and fill both my hands with nails. But my oh my, how slow they are! It takes them forever to nail one board to the other. So while waiting for them to catch up to me, I start hammering on my own with a stone. My grandfather looks down apprehensively from his perch on top of the ladder. He says nothing, but after I slam the stone onto my fingers, he wearily climbs down the ladder and speaks to me in a most persuasive manner.

"*Gae*, Reyzele, *gae*, go. Go and help your grandmother. She is making your favorite, sauerkraut. Go help her make it. You know, when you marry Yossele, you'll have to make your own sauerkraut, so you'd better start learning how to make it."

I am suspicious. I look deeply into my grandfather's eyes to see if he is making fun of me, and I think I can detect a smile lurking somewhere in the corner of his mouth, but I know that my services as succah builder are no longer appreciated. I say nothing while considering my grandfather's suggestion, then decide that it makes a lot of sense. Without another word I run joyfully to tell my grandmother that I am now ready to assist her.

Bursting into the house from the bright sunshine of outdoors, I am in total darkness in my grandmother's cramped kitchen. Gradually I begin to see the light from the tiny window over the cupboard shining on the large stove that covers the entire opposite wall. As shapes and colors come into view, I become aware of the cabbages, large, small and in between, covering all available space. Some are cut in half, others in quarters; some have only the cores left. Stray cabbage leaves of every size and description lie limp on the floor. The pungent smell of cabbage floats around the room, and my mouth starts to water in anticipation of future delights.

An old, weatherbeaten wooden barrel with a large belly encircled by a flat iron band stands in the middle of the kitchen. Around it are my aunts—Libe, Faygl and Shoske. They are packing the cabbage slices that my grandmother cuts on a small table with a large cleaver. They add salt and pinches of sugar, which they alternate with small amounts of water. All are busily working and talking. Their faces are flushed, their hair disheveled, their hands red and rough from their work. No one notices me.

"Bubbe, bubbe," I shout with ear-splitting enthusiasm. "*Der Zayde hot mir gezogt az ikh zol dir helfn.* Grandfather told me to come and help you."

All work stops. My aunts and my grandmother raise their heads and look at me with such disbelief that even in my childishness I sense their terror. I feel the need to defend myself.

"Yes, yes, *der Zayde hot mir gezogt.* Grandfather told me that I have to learn how to make sauerkraut because when I marry Yossele, I will have to make it myself."

I say this with such seriousness and conviction that my aunts burst into peals of laughter. But my grandmother says nothing. Her face is set in a frown, which brings her eyebrows together into one straight line. My grandmother is thinking.

"Well, Raizele," she says slowly, "there is one thing you can do to help. It's a very important thing. In fact, it's one of the most important things in making sauerkraut. But it comes at the very end, so why don't you go out and play, and when we are ready I will call you in."

"Oh, Bubbe!" I say, full of disappointment. "But then I won't learn, and I won't be able to do it myself."

"Don't worry," says my grandmother, "don't worry. When you are ready, we will all come and help you, just as you are helping us."

I stand in the midst of all this exciting activity, unwilling to leave. "Go outside, Raizele, and I promise I will call you," says my grandmother. "I promise by our forefathers Abraham, Isaac and Jacob that I will call you when we are ready."

Sadly I walk out of the house to sit on the steps of our small porch and wait for my grandmother's call. I trust her, especially since she swore by our forefathers.

Time drags; the beautiful October sky is beginning to change colors from pink and blue and indigo to a vivid purple on the edge of the horizon. The air is crisp, and what had been a little breeze is now a cold wind.

I go into the house for the fourth time with an outraged wail. "I'm going home, I'm cold, I'm tired, and I'm hungry. I'm not waiting anymore. I'm going home to my mother."

"Good you came in," says my grandmother in a tired but cheery voice. "Just in time; you came just in time. Now," she adds with a smile, "now we are ready for your most important help."

I look at her, and I look at the barrel, which is covered over with a white cloth. The kitchen is now tidy, and so are my aunts.

"It's all finished," I cry. "It's all finished!"

"No," says my grandmother, "it's definitely not finished." She then takes a round, flat wooden board and places it inside the barrel, completely covering the interior. Then she and my aunts lift up a very large, very round, flat stone and lay it on top of the cover.

"Now," she says as she lifts me up and puts me on top of the stone. "*Yetst, mamele, tants*! Now, darling, dance. Dance and pack the cabbage down so it can ferment and become sour."

I stand there, stunned and not knowing what to do.

"Dance!" call out my aunts with encouragement. "You know how to dance!" With this, they all begin to clap their hands and sing.

At first I just jump a little, but as the music grows louder and merrier, I dance with all my might. I dance for Succos, for sauerkraut, but mostly I dance for pure joy.

A Can of Paint

After hearing this story, a youngster of about nine came up to me to say how much he liked it. "But why," he asked, "didn't your mother dress you in jeans?"

"There were no jeans around in those years," I answered. He looked at me in disbelief.

"Gee," he said at last, "at least you had fun in the outhouse. You know," he added, "if the holes in the outhouse were made the same for everyone, a kid could fall in. Did you ever fall in?"

"Gee," I said, "I never thought of that." Then we all had a good laugh picturing what might have happened, and he walked away, holding his nose. *-RBP*

Having a father in America and living with my mother at home in our shtetl had a profound effect on my early life. It wasn't the big important events that plagued me, except of course that I missed having a father; it was rather the little things that made my childhood life a "river of tears," as they say.

One of these so-called non-consequential situations was that I never looked like any of the other children. I was always dressed up in the latest American fashions. My Aunt Esther, my father's sister, who was instrumental in helping my father come to America, had an eye for fashion. Every few months we received a *pekl*, a bundle from America with clothing that was mostly for me: long silk stockings in an array of colors, sailor blouses with oversized collars that flapped in the wind, accordion-pleated skirts with hip-length blouses, tied with large pink satin bows that always untied and dragged on the ground. There were also little white lace gloves and large ribbon bows, slippery and clumsy, which had to hold in the silky blond curls of my hair, but didn't.

Not only was I the recipient of the latest fashions being worn in the late twenties by the eager immigrants striving for Americanization, but I also received last year's models worn by my cousin Dotty, my aunt's only daughter, who was a few years older than I, and at least a head taller. To this day, I have not forgiven her for the tortures I endured having to wear her hand-me-down clothes.

Clothes became the bane of my existence. I hated them. Not only was I the subject of ridicule by my friends and schoolmates, but my cousin Zisl, who lived next door to us, envied and hated me. Many times I caught her looking at me with a satisfied grin as my mother berated me about my soiled, lost and torn clothing.

Here is just one incident that clearly illustrates the lengths to which a poor innocent child can be driven by the beneficent blessings of a father's generosity from America.

On the morning of my story, my mother had as usual dressed me in all the splendor of the "golden land," with the usual admonition to behave myself and make sure my clothes remained the same "coming in as going out." Miserably, I went outside to stand and sullenly stare at my less fortunate playmates who were merrily romping around in the mud.

Suddenly my cousin Zisl appeared as out of nowhere. She coyly beckoned to me with her long slender finger. Her face, set in a sly grin, showed itself for a moment and then just as quickly disappeared behind the old barn that stood close to our house.

Hesitantly I followed her, not knowing what to expect. As I turned the corner, there stood my cousin Zisl, triumphantly holding a half-filled can of dark green paint.

"*Vu hostu dos gefinen*?" I asked, full of awe and wonder. "Where did you find this?"

"Never mind," says Zisl. "Look," she says, holding up two small bundles of straw bound into shape by several pieces of long narrow strips of fabric. "Brushes, one for you and one for me." She says this with a flourish as she hands me one of her ingenious brushes.

"What are we going to paint?" I ask, almost beside myself with pleasure.

"The old outhouse, of course." She says this with contempt, throwing back her head and pointing to the outhouse. "They just put a new board in and it needs painting."

"But the outhouse has no paint on it," I say, "and anyway, the color green wouldn't match the other wood."

"That's nothing," answers my cousin Zisl. "It's better than having a new board with all the old wood around."

Who was I to argue with such logic? And who looks a gift horse in the mouth, anyway? I was ready and eager to participate in Zisl's uncharacteristically generous offer.

All of a sudden I remember my American dress. "Oh, I can't!" I cry in anguish. "My dress will get dirty, and my mother will kill me."

But Zisl has an answer right on the spot. "You can take off your dress and paint in your underwear."

She says this with such authority that I'm ready to comply then and there. However another obstacle presents itself to me. "Everyone will see me in my underwear," I say, "and it's not nice."

"No they won't, either," says Zisl. "I'll watch out for you. Come on, stop being a cry baby. Let's go." What would you do? So of course, I went.

I joined Zisl in that delicious pastime of painting a brand new, never-before-painted board in a beautiful dark green color. The sun was warm, the little birds sang, the tall grass and wildflowers surrounding our small outhouse danced in the summer breeze to our delightful laughter. Who knew or even cared that the pieces of straw that Zisl had so patiently fashioned into a brush were becoming undone? Who even thought about the falling little strands now soaked in dark green paint, drawing their own design on my white panties and stockings? My dress lay safely on the grass; I had nothing to worry about. With my responsibility attended to, the world was a wonderful place, and for the moment, it was mine, all mine!

Deeply engrossed in our labors, we didn't hear my Aunt Sore-Libe, Zisl's mother, calling her, until her voice reached the volume of a factory whistle. Zisl jumped to attention, leaving me with our illicit treasure, but warning me that she will be back after her chore of bringing her father his lunch.

As time wore on, I grew tired of waiting for Zisl. Besides, it was no fun painting alone. I got myself together, tried to wash the paint off my hands without success. I put the paint and brushes into a piece of burlap I found and hid them in back of Zisl's side of the barn. You see, the barn belonged to both her father and mine, but since my father was in America, my uncle Baruch, her father, had taken possession of our side, too. Zisl and I were always fighting over its ownership.

Tired and disheartened, I put on my dress and go into the house. My mother is busily rendering chicken fat, which crackles and pops out of the pan. The aroma is overpowering. "Mama," I say, "can I have a piece of bread and some *gribenes*? (*Gribenes* is the crusty part of the fat.)

My mother doesn't look up, but warns me not to come too close, as the splash of the fat will burn me. As I stand there in the middle of the room, my mother looks up and views me from head to toe. Her gaze first falls on my white stockings, now painted in an abstract green design unfamiliar to shtetl sensibilities.

"What happened to your stockings?" my mother demands in a hysterical tone. I look down at my feet and feel the earth slipping away from me. "Come here, let me look at you," says my mother, pulling me over to the small window that illuminates our kitchen. Lifting my dress in order to get a better look at my stockings, my mother emits a scream of outraged dismay as she beholds a matching design on my sparkling white bloomers.

"What were you doing? Where were you creeping? How did you get this way? Who gave you the paint? Who were you playing with? What evil spirit inhabits your being? What kind of madness drives you? Look at you, look at you!" screams my mother, as she reaches for the whipping switch that seems to be constantly waiting for me. As far as I can remember, I never felt its sting. My mother really preferred her hands, yet the threat of it was enough to drive me wild.

"It's not my fault; it's not my fault!" I bellow, trembling with fear. "It's not my fault; Zisl did it. Zisl did it!"

"How did she do it?" my mother asks, somewhat calming down. Now I was really on the spot. How could I explain the whole series of events? How could I make her see something that was out of her field of understanding? Then I had it. It struck me like a ton of bricks.

Our shetl of Wysokie-Litewsk was a market town with a large medieval marketplace completely surrounded by a gigantic stone wall. A major portion of the shops and stalls of the shtetl economy were housed in that area. Zisl's father had his butcher stop there, and that was the place to which Zisl had gone to bring him his lunch. A dominant feature of the *brom*, as it was called, was a large iron pump located in the middle of the area, to which the peasants brought their horses to water, washed themselves and their produce, and generally used as a central meeting place. I knew, as did the whole town, that the market pump was being painted, and its color was to be dark green, as it always was. So there it was—my excuse.

"Zisl did it; she pushed me on the pump when I went with her to the *brom* to bring her father his lunch. The pump is still wet," I said. My mother looked at me, trying to make up her mind if what I was saying had any validity. But even when I seemed to appear totally innocent, my mother always found the one area where my input was the cause of my disaster.

"Why did you go to the *brom* without telling me?" scolded my mother in a resigned voice, which I knew indicated defeat for her and victory for me. In other words, she had given up. I had escaped scot-free this time.

A few days later, I accompanied my mother on a shopping trip to the *brom*. As we entered the arched entrance that faced the direction of our house, my mother stopped dead in her tracks, with a look of bewilderment on her face. I looked in the direction of her gaze and saw to my own despair the large iron pump in the middle of the marketplace, shining in all its glory of bright, sunny orange.

My mother did not say a word; she took me by the hand and marched me back home. To describe the punishment inflicted on me would be taking advantage of your good nature. Suffice it to say, I got what she thought I deserved.

Every slap, however, was accompanied by a recitation of what she was not spanking me for. She was not spanking me for going to the *brom* without asking her. She was not spanking me for always fighting with Zisl. She was not spanking me for being such a *vilde khayeh*, a wild animal. She was not spanking me for always soiling and tearing my clothes. She was not spanking me for always being disobedient.

What she was spanking me for was that her child, on whom she lavished all her time and love and affection, was going to grow up to be the world's biggest liar.

Now I ask you, how could she know I was going to become a storyteller?

It's Only a Purim Shpiel

There is a section of this story in which I enumerate all the delicacies that my aunts and grandmother prepare for the holiday. I relate how I pestered them to let me help them in all they attempted to do. Then I ask in the story, "So what could my grandmother do?"

At one performance, before I could give the solution, a man yelled out from the audience, "Give you a good spanking!"

"Yes," I answered him, "but then you wouldn't have a story." *-RBP*

Purim is coming—you can smell it in the air. Even the snow, hard-packed and glistening in the sun, feels it and cries a little, making puddles in the well-worn pathways. Poor snow; it knows that if Purim is here, Pesakh can't be far behind, and it brings with it the sweet and glorious spring. Soon the rains will come and turn everything to mud. Purim is coming, and the long winter with its boring nights and icy days is just about over.

There is lots of gay talk in my grandparents' house. Everyone is busy preparing for Purim. Everyone is busy writing, making lists. My grandmother and my mother are making a list of all the ingredients needed to make and bake all the Purim delicacies. *Teiglakh*, cakes, tarts, cookies in all shapes and sizes, scones filled with prune jam or currants and, of course, those tasty, gooey hamentashen. My aunts Liebe and Shushke are compiling lists of who is to receive *shalakhmones*, gifts of delicacies exchanged by one family with another. My mother and my grandmother really have the final say on this matter and will no doubt rearrange the names.

My uncle Avrom-Layb has enlisted the services of my Aunt Fiegel to help him write a new version of the Purim *shpiel*, which will then have to be presented to the Dramatic Society for approval. My uncle is a *gantzer makher*, a big wheel in this society, which can boast of the best and the brightest young people of the shtetl.

This dramatic group was originally organized to perform Bible stories like "The Selling of Joseph," or the story of Hanukkah or Purim, told through satire. But it expanded its repertoire with the influx of more educated, more enlightened young actors. It now performed Shakespeare, Ibsen, Chekhov in Yiddish. There was always a charge to attend a performance, and the money would go to support the town library. During Purim, however, the actors put the money given to them by the householders in whose homes the story of "The Megila of Esther" was performed into a fund for the needy of the shtetl, for Passover provisions. And I, Raizelle Kolner, was part of this troupe!

How did this all come about, you may ask? Well, if you'll give me a moment of your time, I'll tell you about it.

Since my father was in America, and although my mother and I lived in our own apartment, my mother, who was the oldest of four sisters and one brother, practically lived in my grandparents' house. And, since she was always there, where should I be if not with her? I was the only grandchild and smart for my age, so I became the pest of the entire household. But before holidays, even those saintly people gave up on me. I was constantly underfoot, involving myself in all the intricate preparations that were being planned for the holiday celebration.

Imagine having a child of six declaring loudly that she wants to mix the poppy seeds with the honey for the *hamentashen*, knead the dough for the *challah*, fill the scones with prunes and press the cookies!

Well, my grandmother is no one's fool, so she sends me off to my Uncle Avrom-Layb, whom I adore. And no small wonder, because to me he has all the qualifications of what God must be like. Tall, blond, handsome, full of fun and stories. Besides which he is a hero to all the young ladies of the town. Wasn't he always the most important character in the plays? Didn't he always have the biggest parts? Boy, I sure was lucky to have him as my uncle. (A fact which my cousin Zisl, on my father's side, used to tell me whenever she went with me to my grandparents' house.)

So what was Avrom-Layb going to do with me? As usual, he hit on a most ingenious plan. Since I had a very loud voice and was not ashamed to use it, he decided to dress me up as a Purim shpieler, a little raggedy clown with a *grogger*, a noisemaker, in my hand with which I called the people gathered to see the Purim shpiel to attention. When I had them listening, my uncle would give me a sign, and then I would call out loud and clear, "*Zietye Yiden sha un shtil—mir haben on de Purim shpiel!*"

Then after the play was over, I would bow graciously to the audience and say, "*Hynt iz Purim, morgen is oys—Git undz a grosen un varft undz aroys!* Today is Purim, tomorrow it's done—Give us a penny and tell us be gone!"

I would then take my cone-shaped hat, which had a large red pompom on it, turn it upside down, and use it as a bag to collect the money. The Purim shpiel was always a hit, and my participation in it was not only an asset to the company, but it was also a great relief to my mother and grandmother, because I wasn't underfoot.

The last Purim shpiel I was involved in was a most memorable occasion. Actually, it is really the reason why I am telling you this story.

For that year's Purim shpiel, my uncle had a brand-new scenario on the megilla story. That year, it seemed that the beautiful Esther had a heretofore unknown boyfriend who was broken-hearted that she had allowed herself to be talked into applying for that beauty contest by her uncle Mordekhai. Now that she had actually won it, he decided to confront Mordekhai himself about Esther's Ahashverus. My uncle Avrom-Layb, who always played Mordekhai, was now playing the broken-hearted boyfriend.

There was, however, a subplot to that Purim shpiel. You see, my uncle was himself courting a girl who was considered to be a great beauty. Not only was she beautiful, but her father was one of the wealthiest men in the shtetl. He did not look too kindly on this modern notion of his daughter going out with young men, especially those whose *yikhes* (status) was not to his liking.

I had often heard my family joke about my uncle's romance with this rich girl, whose name by the way was also Esther. They did not take it seriously. My uncle, after all, was all of seventeen years old. But to him, it was a painful situation.

Well, to continue with the Purim shpiel. After going to several homes and performing this original version of the Megilla, which by the way was greeted with much fun and laughter, we finally came to the home of Reb Fievel Rosenfeld, the owner of the one factory in the shtetl, a tannery in which my grandfather worked. He also happened to be Esther's father.

Reb Fievel, his wife and children, along with other family members, uncles, aunts, nieces, nephews and cousins, were seated around a large table, heavily laden with the best that Purim offered. The beautiful Esther, my uncle's love, was seated at her father's side.

When the play began and Reb Fievel became aware of what was now going on in the Purim shpiel, he got up from the table and asked if he could take over the role of Mordekhai. Since everyone knew the traditional story, this was not such a far-fetched request. However, with this year's additional character of the boyfriend, everyone waited for the unexpected. The actors all looked at one another with meaningful glances. What was now going to take place was a play within a play. Avrom-Layb was now going to plead his own case. But how should I, a child of six, understand all this?

Reb Rievel was in great humor, enjoying every minute of my uncle's pleading for his Esther. Everyone was in stitches, everyone was laughing, but not me. I forgot all about Purim, I forgot all about the play, all I heard was my uncle's voice, all I felt was my uncle's pain. Then when Reb Fievel called his daughter Esther over and asked her if she would rather marry this penniless boyfriend instead of the great king Ahasverus and thereby save her people, and when she answered without a moment's hesitation that she would rather marry the king, I jumped up, ran over to my uncle and cried out with all the soul in me, "Don't feel bad, Avrom-Layb. You don't need her. Just wait for me to grow up, and I will marry you, I promise, I promise!" I then started to cry as if my heart would break.

My uncle grabbed me in his arms, hugged me close, and to the accompaniment of the raucous laughter of everyone in the room, I buried my head deeply into his shoulder.

"Raizelle," said my uncle, "it's only a Purim *shpiel*!"

Rolling Around on the Stove

When I told this story to people before performing it professionally, many of them couldn't understand what rolling around on the stove meant. After I explained it to them, they said, "That's the first sexy story I ever heard about the shtetl." *–RBP*

My grandmother bought a new stove. It was the talk of the entire family. My grandfather was continually grumbling about my grandmother's extravagance. My aunts and my mother were very excited over it, and my uncle Avron-Layb kept making all kinds of off-color jokes about it, some of which I didn't understand.

However, there was one thing he said I understood very well. He said, "How great it would be to be able to roll around on the stove." All he needed, he said, was a peasant girl.

My grandparents yelled at him for saying this, but my aunts laughed. I didn't know why my grandparents were angry, or why my aunts thought it was funny, but I thought it was a wonderful idea, so I asked him.

His answer was just as mysterious. He said, "When you grow up, Rayzele, you will know what I mean."

And then he laughed, which made my grandfather really angry. And he said, "Is that what you say to a child? Shame on you!"

My grandmother's old stove was made of clay just like ours and everyone else's. It was situated in the kitchen, and there was a big connecting pipe to the pot-belly stove in the main room of the house.

It didn't give much heat in the winter, because it was always cold and everyone had to wear a real warm sweater or a shawl. Our houses were different than the peasant houses because they had only one room and their stove was right in the middle of it. I know, because one time my mother took me to a peasant family for a few days. We all slept in little alcoves against the wall of the big room, and we had a curtain to draw when we went to sleep. Their stove was built up high on one side and had a kind of platform on top so someone could sleep there on real cold nights, but I didn't know that they rolled around on it or why they would.

My grandmother had ordered her new stove from Warsaw. It was supposed to be the latest style. It was made of tile. The main part of it was in the kitchen and then extended into the big main room, where you could sit against it in the winter to keep good and warm. It was also built about five feet high on one side with a platform. There were places to put your toes if you wanted to climb up. It looked absolutely grand.

As soon as it was installed, I wanted to climb up there and see what was so funny about rolling around on the stove.

When I tried to get up there, everyone in the family was adamant in their refusal to let me go. It was too dangerous for a child to attempt the climb, they said. But I was determined. There was too much mystery about the top of that stove for me to forget about it. I knew if I waited, the opportunity would present itself.

I didn't have to wait long. My mother and grandmother had gone to visit a sick neighbor, all my aunts were away, and my uncle was at a meeting of the Theatrical Society. I was left in the care of my grandfather, who was reading a newspaper. I was busy drawing, but when I heard my grandfather start to snore, I knew my chance had come.

I climbed up the first two indentations without too much trouble; the third one was rather tricky, as there was nothing to hold on to. But the fourth one was really scary. By the fifth one, I was sorry I had ever started the whole thing. I felt I would absolutely fall if I tried to go down again, and so I closed my eyes, and with all my strength I lifted myself up to grab the edge of the platform.

I was on the verge of tears when I finally tumbled onto the top. I was surprised to find that it was lower than the edge. I guessed it was made that way to keep a person from falling off when they were rolling around. After resting for a while and looking from my perch to see that my grandfather was still snoring, I started to roll around. I rolled around for a while, but I didn't see what was so great about it. My back started to hurt, as there was nothing soft to lean on, and it had become quite boring. I wanted to come down, but I was too frightened.

Meanwhile my mother and grandmother came back and started to look for me, as I seemed to be nowhere around. My grandfather couldn't figure out where I had gone. Everyone started to look for me, calling my name over and over again. My three aunts returned home and found my mother almost beside herself with worry. My aunts ran out of the house to the darkened road to see if I had gone out. And I, lying flat on the top of the stove, began to whimper. I knew somehow I would be saved, but I also knew my mother would surely kill me.

When my uncle came home, the whole house was in an uproar. After finding out I was missing, he joined in the search. Seeing my uncle gave me a little courage, as he always protected me against my mother's wrath. I peeked out from the top of the stove and softly whispered his name. Somehow he heard me above the lamentations of my mother and grandmother. He looked up and saw me, tears silently running down my face. Without saying a word, he climbed up and brought me down.

I cannot describe the anger in everyone's face when they saw me. I cannot describe the fear I felt as I saw my mother advancing towards me with what could only be described as pure fury.

My uncle was still holding me, and I clung to him for dear life. He held off my mother with one hand and somehow calmed her down.

"Now tell us, Rayzele," he said, "why did you climb up there when everyone told you that you are not allowed to do it?"

"I know I shouldn't have climbed up, but you said it would be great fun rolling around on the stove, and I couldn't wait until I grew up. I wanted to try it for myself. And I want to tell you it was no fun at all, and it wasn't worth the climb."

I saw smiles on everyone's faces. I didn't know why they were smiling, but at least my mother didn't kill me.

The Sunflower and the Alphabet

After hearing this story, a little girl and her mother came up to me to tell me how much they liked it. The little girl then shyly pulled on the mother's hand to remind her of something. The mother said, "Oh yes, Jenny told me to tell you she has a secret she would like to share with you."

"Great," I said. "I love secrets."

I bent down, and the little girl whispered in my ear, "I also talk to my flowers." And then she gave me a big, smudgy kiss. *-RBP*

Autumn is a wonderful time of year in the little Jewish village where I was born. My father had gone to America when I was six months old, and my mother and I were waiting for him to send for us. Meanwhile we lived right near both my mother's and father's family, whom I loved and who loved me. But mostly I had Zisl, my cousin, who was my age and was the daughter of my father's brother. We were constantly together, loving or fighting.

Zisl and I, who are now quite grown up—we are seven years old—decide that autumn is the time of year we like most of all. It is full of excitement. The Jewish months of Elul, Tishri and Kheshvan, which are our months of September, October and a little bit of November, have lots of things going on all the time. Gathering the fruit and vegetables from the garden, cooking, pickling and preserving food for the winter. There is also lots of fixing of houses and roofs and barns so that people and animals will be warm in the cold weather.

But most of all, autumn has many holidays: Rosh Hashona, Yom Kippur, Succos, Simkhes-Toyre. This time of year is very busy for our family, but it is also busy for Zisl and me. Since everyone is working preparing for the holidays so that they don't shame the holy days by not having a clean house, or new clothes, or the right kind of food, they send us on all kinds of errands. They send us to bring this, or take that, or help carry or go into, or creep under, or watch out, or get out of the way. Children do lots of work that is hardly noticed by older people; they think we just play all the time!

Zisl and I just love the autumn. The weather is so beautiful. It isn't as hot as it is in summer. The sky is crystal clear, and when the sun goes down, it paints the sky in so many colors of pink and purple, blue and gold. But most of all we love the flowers in autumn. The wild flowers that grow everywhere in all the colors of the rainbow, tall and short, big and small. Zisl and I always pick them and bring them home so our house can look as beautiful as the fields outside.

There was one flower that I loved more than any other. It was a very large sunflower that grew in the back of the house of a little old lady whose name was Bubbe Zelde, Grandma Zelde. Bubbe Zelde was my Hebrew teacher. She taught me Loshn Koydesh, the holy language, the language in which you pray and read from the *siddur*, the prayer book. I started going to Bubbe Zelde three times a week just after Simkhes-Toyre.

Zisl already knew her alphabet, because her older brothers taught her. They were my relatives too, even though they were just my cousins, but they never taught me! At first I didn't want to go because it was autumn and there were so many other exciting things to do, but my mother said I had to. She said that since Simkhes-Toyre celebrated the complete reading of the Toyre, which took a whole year to finish, it was a *mitzvah*, a good deed, for a child to start to learn to read it at the same time that Klal Yisroel, all the Jewish people, started their rereading of it in synagogue. She also said it was a sin for a child my age not to know how to daven, recite the prayers, and since I was against all sins and since I didn't want Zisl to be the only one to know how to read, I went.

Bubbe Zelde's house is very small, just like she is, and it leans to one side, just like she does. The floor in the room in which I read my letters is very slanty. Since Bubbe Zelde needs a lot of light in order to see, we go up hill to the one little window in back of the room. And who is peering into the window all bright and golden but that wonderful sunflower.

How can I keep my mind on my lesson when the sunflower keeps nodding to me with its one big golden eye calling, "Come out little girl, come out and play." Bubbe Zelde complains to my mother that I don't pay attention to my lesson but keep looking out of the window.

My mother wants to know what is so interesting outside, so I tell her about the sunflower. "Sunflowers don't speak to little children," says my mother, "all they do is make sunflower seeds to be roasted and eaten during the winter." Then of course I tell Zisl about the sunflower calling to me, and Zisl looks at me and smiles her know-it-all smile and says, "Oh, you're always making up stories." She also doesn't believe me. However, when I tell my Aunt Shushke, my mother's sister, the one who always reads stories to me, that the sunflower does call me to come out, she says it could be so. Actually she says, "What the sunflower is really saying is that it too would like to learn the *alef-beyz*, the alphabet, because it too would like to learn to daven, to read the prayers." My Aunt Shushke knows about such things because she loves flowers more than anyone. But when I repeat this to Zisl she only laughs and says, "Seeing is believing."

So the very next time I go for my lesson, I don't look out the window but try hard to learn my alef-beyz. I can't wait to rush out and repeat what I have learned to the sunflower, but not before I get a good lick of honey from Bubbe Zelde. Bubbe Zelde always gives me a lick of honey after my lesson because she says that studying Toyre is as sweet as honey, and the honey in my mouth would help to remind me of that.

Running behind the house I see Zisl waiting for me. "I've come to see your talking sunflower," she says.

"Well," I say, "You can watch, but you can't say a word." Zisl nods. I repeat my lesson to the sunflower, "*Kometz alef oh, kometz beys boh, kometz gimel goh, komets daled doh.*" After the sunflower nods its head to me once or twice, I know it has learned the lesson. Then I also give it a lick of honey, which I still have on my tongue. Zisl is still unimpressed. "It takes time to learn," I assure her. "Just you wait and see."

And so the sunflower and I study together for several weeks, until one day as it is getting colder, I notice the gold fading from the face of the sunflower. It is turning a kind of light brown and starting to drop its head lower and lower. When I look closer into its face, I see it is separating into little diagonal boxes. I think that perhaps it is getting sick. I confide this to Zisl.

"Maybe it can't take all that learning," she says with a sly look in her eyes. "Maybe we should go to your aunt Shushke and ask her."

We both hurry over to my grandmother's house to report this to my aunt. "All this learning is making the sunflower sick," I say. "It's getting to look old and wrinkled." Zisl nods her head in agreement.

"No, no," says my Aunt Shushke. "What is really happening is that the sunflower is storing all the letters into its seeds.

"Since letters when put together become words, and words put together become sentences, and sentences put together become paragraphs, and many paragraphs make up a story, the sunflower is actually storing a story within itself which will be told when people sit around in the evenings cracking sunflower seeds and telling stories." I can see by the look on Zisl's face that she is interested in what my aunt has told us. I am very impressed.

So, after my next Hebrew lesson, I run to the sunflower. Perhaps I can see a few of the sentences that are part of the story.

"Here is a lick of honey to help you remember the letters I taught you," I say to the sunflower, sticking out my tongue as I had done so many times before. All of a sudden, I hear a loud buzzing sound, and I feel an agonizing piercing pain engulf my entire tongue as a bumble bee hurriedly leaves both me and the sunflower. My tongue swells and swells and seems to expand into gigantic proportions in my mouth. Hysterical, I run home to my mother.

"That's what you get for sticking your tongue where it doesn't belong," says my mother as she tries to soothe me in her own inimitable manner. Later that day, almost everyone in my family comes to see me and tries to make me feel better, but my tongue stays swollen all that night.

The next day my cousin Zisl comes to visit. She tries to cheer me up by singing and dancing, and she doesn't stop talking. She keeps asking all kinds of questions about the sunflower, even though she knows I can hardly open my mouth to answer her. My mother sends her home so we both can have a little peace and quiet. After a few days, my tongue feels much better, so I go to Bubbe Zelde's house for another lesson.

As usual, I go to the sunflower to see how it is doing. But it isn't there! I see its stem, but its head is missing! I'm beside myself with grief. Where could it have gone? My flower with whom I shared so much has disappeared, and I will never hear those stories stored in its seeds. Slowly I go to Zisl's house to tell her of my tragedy. She is sympathetic, but it doesn't seem to bother her too much. It's not her flower, I think to myself. She is not the one who loved it or took care of it, or taught it. I go home very sad and lonely.

But how long can you stay sad and lonely when the first snow of winter has just fallen and the world has become so white and clean? Winter has arrived while I wasn't looking, with its cold winds and its long nights. Pretty soon Hanukkah will be here, with lots of people coming to our house for the celebration. We will light the Hanukkah candles, eat *latkes*, play cards and *driedel*, get Hanukkah presents, and what I loved most of all, tell lots of stories.

A few days before Hanukkah, Zisl comes to my house carrying a bag, which she gives me with a shy smile. "Here is your sunflower," she says, looking very ashamed. "I had my mother dry the flower and roast its seeds. I ate lots and lots of seeds, but I still can't tell stories the way your Aunt Shushke does. So I guess eating sunflower seeds doesn't work for everyone, even though yours knew the alphabet."

At first I didn't know what to say, because Zisl looked so unhappy. Then I started to laugh, and that made Zisl laugh, and we laughed and laughed together. I laughed because I had my sunflower back, and I laughed because I know that you have to hear stories first before you can tell them, and I also laughed that at last I could do something that Zisl couldn't do better than me. But why Zisl laughed, I never knew.

Zisl's Hanukkah Lamp

After I wrote this story, my husband suggested that we try to follow Zisl's suggestion of lighting half a potato with a string and some oil. But we couldn't do it. We figured we must have needed kerosene or something. Then it hit me: Here I was, all these years later, still doing what Zisl told me. *–RBP*

My cousin Zisl and I were constant companions—not that we particularly liked one another. In fact, there were times when we actually hated each other. But since we lived next door to each other, had the same relatives, played the same games, liked getting into the same kind of trouble, we had no other recourse than to spend every possible moment together.

Zisl was the one with the ideas, and I always the willing follower. Let me tell you about one of Zisl's ideas that took place on the third night of Hanukkah on a cold Friday afternoon before sundown. Mothers are always busy at that time, because they are preparing for Shabbes. After sundown, no work is allowed, and on this particular Friday, it was also Hanukkah.

I was at home with my mother waiting for the sun to start going down so we could light the Hanukkah candles before the Shabbes candles were lit when Zisl knocked on our door. She said she had something important to tell me, and with a nod of her head she indicated that we go into the bedroom. Then without saying a word, she pulls a potato out of her pocket, winks at me, and puts her fingers to her lips.

"Shhh—," says Zisl in a whisper. "Don't ask questions. Just tell your mother you want a piece of bread with lots of butter on it and meet me outside." I am used to receiving mysterious instructions from Zisl, and I know something interesting is about to happen.

My mother doesn't understand my sudden love for butter, because I usually hate it, but she is glad to be rid of me. Out I go into the cold and windy street to meet Zisl.

Solemnly we both march into the cold barn, which stands a few feet away from the house. The barn belonged to both my father and Zisl's father, but since my father was in America, Zisl's father had taken complete possession of it and used it as a storage place. Zisl and I were always fighting over its ownership. The barn was one of our favorite places to play.

As soon as we are inside, Zisl puts her potato on the floor and then pulls out of her pocket several pieces of string, three matches, a handful of chicken fat wrapped in a piece of cloth and an old, broken, rusty knife.

"What are we going to do here," I want to know, "cook the potato with a match?"

"*Oy, biztu a nar*, boy, are you a fool," says Zisl. "What we are going to do is have our own Hanukkah celebration. No one ever lets me have a turn to light the Hanukkah candles or say the *brokhe*, the blessing, so we are going to do it ourselves."

"Do you know the whole *brokhe*? I don't, but I know the story of Hanukkah," I say. "I bet you don't know it!"

"I do so," says Zisl, "but what is it?"

"Well, once there was a very bad king who came into the Jewish land of Israel, and he told the people that they can't be Jews anymore, only Greeks. Well, they didn't like that at all, and they got very angry. So, they had a war, and the Jewish people won because they had Judah Maccabee. After they won, they cleaned out the Temple in Jerusalem, which had pigs in it. Then they wanted to light the menorah, so they found a little jar of oil enough for one day, but the menorah burned for eight days. It was a miracle! So that's why Hanukkah is eight days long."

"I knew it all the time," says Zisl. I knew she didn't, but I didn't want to fight about it now.

"With what are you going to make the Hanukkah lamp, and where are the candles?" I ask. "*Oy biztu a nar*, boy, are you a fool," says Zisl. "What do you think all these things are for? Look, first I cut the potato in half, then I dig out a couple of holes and put the butter from your bread, with the chicken fat I brought into the holes so we can have the oil."

"What," I say, "are you going to put the butter with the chicken fat together? That's *treif,* it's not kosher, it's not allowed. It's a sin, and I'm not playing."

"*Oy biztu a nar,*" says my cousin Zisl. "Do you think I don't know that? We are going to make one Hanukkah lamp *milkhig*, dairy, and the other *flayshig*, for meat." That plan calms my fear, but another problem presents itself to me. "How are you going to make oil out of butter and chicken fat?"

"We don't have to," says Zisl. "We'll just smear some fat on the strings so they'll be like the wicks we use in our kerosene lamps, and then they'll burn. My brother Shameh says that kerosene is just like fat, only it's not for eating." Well, if Shameh says so, it must be so, because Shameh, Zisl's oldest brother, is the most handsome boy in the world, so I'm convinced!

"*Nu*, well," I say, "let's start already. It's cold in here, and it will soon be Shabbes." Zisl smears one string with butter, the other with chicken fat. She then digs out three little holes in each potato half, cuts each string into threes, and inserts a piece of string into each hole. Now we are going to light the string and say the *brokhe.* Zisl begins, "*Baruch atah adoshem eloheynu melech ha olam, asher kiddishanu....*" Zisl is saying the blessing, while she tries to light the greasy string with a match. It doesn't light! The match goes out. She tries again with the second match. It too goes out. Now we have only one match left.

"Let me try," I say. "You already had two chances." Zisl refuses. "It's my idea, and these are my matches," says Zisl.

"It's not fair, it's not fair," I say. You did everything, and I didn't do anything." Now I'm ready to start crying, which is my usual response to Zisl's bossy ways.

"You're always crying," says Zisl, but she hands me the match which she has, however, lit.

I take the burning match and try to light the string. It doesn't light, and I see that the fire is about to reach my fingers, so I grab the rag that Zisl's chicken fat was in and wrap it around the match. The burning match together with the rag fell from my hand and, wonder of wonders, the rag starts to burn.

"Great," we both say. Now we'll be able to light the string, because the cloth will burn for a long time.

It may have been great, but we two heroines do not notice that the floor of the barn is covered with fine sawdust, which is now starting to burn. All we know is that the string does not light, but the barn is getting warmer and starting to smell delicious. By the time we realized what was happening, we were too frightened to do anything but run out of the barn.

"Come on, come on, let's tell somebody that the barn is on fire!" I cry, pulling on Zisl's arms. But Zisl doesn't listen, and for once it's Zisl who starts crying.

"No, no," she screams though her tears, "I can't, I can't, I'll be killed." Without even turning around, Zisl runs into the vegetable garden and hides behind the lima bean poles. As usual I follow her, and the fire burns merrily in the barn.

By the time it was noticed, smoke was pouring out of the cracks in the door and walls of the barn. People began to run and shout, "*Pashar, pashar*, fire, fire! *Kumt aroyse de shtall brent*, come out, come out, the barn is burning!"

People knocked on windows, on doors, calling for help to put out the fire. Everyone runs to see what is going on. Zisl's brothers run with pails to the pond, which is a short distance from the house for water, but the pond is frozen. The ice has to be broken through. Someone shouts, "*Reeft de Pozharne Commande*, call the fire brigade!" Other young men have by now formed a bucket brigade from the pond to the barn. But many of the older men do not move to do anything.

"*Es is shein Shabbes, mit tor nisht arbettin, loze es brennen*, it is now Shabbes, no work is allowed, let it burn." They just stand there, looking at the barn and praying.

My mother and Zisl's mother have also run into the street. "*Vee zanen de kinder*, where are the children?" they asked one another. "Raizel, Zisl," they shout, running this way and that. Zisl and I, hiding behind the lima bean poles, tremble with fear and guilt.

Not finding us, my Aunt Sorre-Liebe, Zisl's mother, suddenly lets out an earth-shaking scream, as it occurs to her that we could be in the burning barn. My mother, hearing my aunt screaming and having come to the same conclusion, also starts to scream and run towards the barn.

My Uncle Borakh, Zisl's father, who is now directing the fire brigade, runs towards my mother to restrain her. My mother is like a wild woman trying to get into the barn.

"*De kinder, de kinder*," she shrieks. "The children are burning up in the barn!" This causes a complete panic. My aunt faints, the women and children start shrieking, all the older men including the very pious ones stop praying and join in putting out the flames. Lives are involved, and life comes before all else.

My Uncle Borakh, making sure that both my mother and aunt are being taken care of, starts to look for us. He is sure that we are not in the barn. He knows that Zisl and I are smart enough not to allow ourselves to be trapped there. Knowing that we often play in the vegetable garden, he goes directly there and finds us shivering with cold and fright.

When he walked into sight holding us each by the hand, a cheer went up from all the worried neighbors, friends and relatives. Zisl and I walked toward our mothers as ones being led to their execution, but to our amazement, we were both gathered into their ams, hugged and kissed. They were so happy to see us.

It wasn't until the next day after we told our story and, of course, when the Shabbes was over, that punishment was applied. Zisl and I could not sit down for weeks. We were shunned by one and all and were not allowed to play with each other for what seemed like forever.

When we did get together two days later, we went to examine the burned-out barn, and guess what we found. Guess? Zisl's Hanukkah lamps. The two potato halves were now blackened and very nicely roasted. So we ate them.

The Wedding in the Cemetery

I told this story for Halloween at Three Apples Festival in Massachusetts, along with several other tellers who told scary stories. After the performances, we stood talking to the middle school students in the audience. Most of them said they didn't believe my story. Try as I might, I couldn't convince them that it was true!

–RBP

Cemeteries have always played a major role in the ghostly tales that haunted the dreams of both children and adults in my little village in Belarus, and for good reason.

To the people of my town, the cemetery was an ever-present active component of their lives. There lay not only the physical remains of their beloved departed relatives interred for their final rest, but it was also a place where one went to commune with the spirits of all of one's ancestors, starting with our forefathers Abraham, Isaac and Jacob.

One went there not only to petition those holy ones to intercede in one's behalf, for they were the closest to God, but also to invite, beg, pardon, ask advice or placate less illustrious souls who were no longer housed in their bodies, yet who were very much alive to the people of my town.

Going past the cemetery at night meant exposing oneself to the many wandering souls, good and evil, who were busily going about their business of participating in the harried, worried, dangerous world of the living. As a child, I was scared out of my wits when passing the cemetery day or night. Who in their right mind would feel comfortable with all those roving ghosts who knew all, saw all, and made their own demands?

My grandmother, wanting to calm my fears by making me familiar with her own childhood experiences with roving spirits in the cemetery, told the whole family this story one afternoon after the Shabbes meal.

"Once as a child, I was taken to a wedding in the cemetery. You see, there was a terrible outbreak of cholera in our town. Why it suddenly should happen in the middle of the winter was a mystery. Usually an epidemic like this came in the summertime. What was going on? So it was decided that some spirit was probably offended and was causing this catastrophe. What could be done to placate this evil spirit?

"The Rebbe was consulted. The Rebbe was a little uncomfortable about blaming what was happening on an evil spirit. You see, he was a very learned man, not only in Toyre, but also in *veltikhe zakhen*, worldly affairs, and he tried to tell the people that cholera was a sickness that sometimes happens. He did not think that any evil spirit had anything to do with it, but the people of our town wouldn't hear of it. They knew that it was an offended soul that needed to be placated.

"The Rebbe was asked if he could arrange a marriage that would take place in the cemetery. The spirits like nothing better than a wedding, and the townspeople were sure that it would please the soul that was causing all the trouble. Many people related stories they had heard from their grandfathers or grandmothers of similar incidents and how a wedding on the cemetery was the only thing that helped. The Rebbe definitely did not like the whole idea. Who in their right mind would agree to be married in a graveyard? However, he could not dissuade the crowd of people that had come to him in fear and determination.

"They had an idea, they said. There were several orphans in town who would be only too glad to have a wedding arranged for them, especially if it was paid for by the community, and especially if a handsome dowry was also provided. They named the pair. The Rebbe thought it over and decided that it would really be a *mitzvah*, a good deed, to help two unfortunate young people enter the holy state of matrimony and also have a little money to start a respectable life.

"And so it was agreed that the wedding would take place the very next week. No one wanted to take a chance on waiting, as the cholera was spreading rapidly throughout the town's population. The two orphans were notified. They were young and poor, and all alone in the world, and they saw this as an opportunity. However, fear gripped their souls. To be married in the cemetery was not something to look forward to.

"The whole town began the preparations for the wedding. There was the matter of collecting the money for the dowry, no easy job, seeing that almost everyone in the shtetl was on the verge of poverty themselves.

"Then clothes had to be bought, both for the bride and groom, as those they had were absolutely threadbare. Then there was the matter of some refreshments and also some wine for the *l'chaim* and the *kiddush*. Everyone was invited. In fact, those who did not attend would be severely criticized. Also, everyone was to bring their children, for next to weddings, the spirits like children best.

"The day arrived, a Friday afternoon. My mother and father took me, and my youngest brother, and we joined the rest of the town at the cemetery near the grave of the bride's mother. Surely she would intercede with this avenging spirit if nothing else moved him.

"My brother and I held onto each other and to our parents for dear life. It felt so scary, so spooky, so filled with dread. Would the evil spirit show itself? What would it look like? It was all fearsome and exciting at the same time.

"The wedding canopy was set up. The bride and groom, held tightly under both arms, were led under it. The bride looked as if she were about to faint any moment. The groom was pale, and you could see he was shaking with fright. The elders of the town covered their heads with prayer shawls turning this way and that, chanting wailing prayers that turned our blood to water and sent chills up and down our spines. The bride and groom huddled together, while old women shrieked and cried, begging the evil one to depart from us all. We children standing glued to our parents were absolutely sure that we could see the many ghostly apparitions coming out of their graves to attend the wedding.

"The Rebbe was just about to start the ceremony, when suddenly, from several directions of the cemetery, there came the most unearthly screams one can imagine. They went on for a moment or two, and then broke into raucous ghoulish laughter. All the assembled crowd stood there panic-stricken, and then started running for their lives. The bride fainted; the groom had to be held up to keep from falling. Only the Rebbe covered his head with his prayer shawl and continued rocking back and forth with hands folded in deep prayer.

"Much to my horror, I found that I was wetting my pants as I ran. This made me shriek even more than most.

"We finally stopped running when we were outside the cemetery. There, we all stood waiting for the Rebbe to appear with the bride and groom. After what seemed an eternity, the Rebbe came out with the young couple and several older men, gripping four struggling young men by the arms. The Rebbe then explained that these young men had been the ones making those horrible sounds. A riot almost broke out, because some of the townspeople wanted to beat them up. When things quieted down, one of the young men was allowed to tell the people why they did such a terrible thing—not only disrupting the wedding, but also putting the town in greater danger and revenge from the evil spirits.

"One of the young men started laughing, but when he saw how angry the people were, he stopped and spoke seriously. He told them that they were backward and superstitious. That cholera was a sickness that came from unclean water and not evil spirits. He said that he and his friends wanted to prove that they were all afraid of things that do not exist.

"But the people were still very angry and urged the Rebbe to take action against the young men through the Rabbinical Court. The Rebbe agreed, but said that now the important thing was to complete the marriage ceremony, as the bride and groom had already suffered enough. And so they were married right there, outside of the cemetery gate. No one wanted to go back to the graves.

"The cholera epidemic subsided, so the evil spirits must have gotten what they wanted. But you know, the young men were right; cholera does come from unclean water.

"As far as the spirits are concerned," concluded my grandmother with a broad smile, "let them rest in peace."

The Prophet Elijah, My Uncle and Me

When I first started working on this story, I was very interested in getting down all the preparations for the holiday, because those preparations meant more to me than the holiday itself. I truly missed them here in America. *–RBP*

I was born in a little Jewish town called a shtetl, in what is now the country of Belarus, a long, long time ago. But I still remember many things about my old home. My father left for America when I was only six months old. While my mother and I waited to join him, we lived with my mother's family. I especially remember the many wonderful holidays spent with them.

Pesakh, Passover, was the holiday I liked best, because there was so much to do to prepare for it, and I loved to be able to help. You see, I was almost grown up by then. I was seven years old.

The Pesakh I want to tell you about still makes my heart beat with excitement, because of what happened when Elijah the Prophet, my uncle, and I upset the Seder and got into trouble with the whole family.

It was an early spring morning. Outside, the sun shone on everything, the houses, the trees, the alleyways. Inside, the women of my family were sitting around my grandmother's large wooden table sewing. A lamp lit up the room, as the windows still had their winter shutters on them.

Suddenly the door opens, and in comes my young Uncle Avrom-Layb. Spreading his arms out like an actor on a stage, he recites in a loud voice, "For lo, the winter is passed, the rain is over and gone, the flowers appear on the earth. Last night, I think I heard the voice of the turtle dove, and it said it was time to start preparing for Pesakh. When do we start taking off the shutters and let in spring, wonderful spring?"

My three aunts look up from their sewing, start laughing, and begin clapping their hands and singing one of our favorite Pesakh songs from the Haggada, the prayer book we recite from during the Seder, called Dayenu.

"Stop the commotion," shouts my bubbe, my grandmother.

"Stop fooling around with words from our holy books," thunders my zayde, my grandfather. "You are no longer children to carry on like this."

"I'm a child," I say. "I'm only seven years old. Can I carry on?"

"Are you trying to outdo your uncle Avrom-Layb with his jokes and his nonsense?" says my bubbe, and my zayde just smiles.

My uncle Avrom-Layb is my favorite person in the whole world. He is always fooling around making everyone laugh, especially me. My grandparents are always scolding him, but that never stops him. He is their youngest child and their only son, and I think he is their favorite, too.

I am thrilled by what my uncle said, because now it is time to start working on all the things that have to be done to make ready for Pesakh.

"In ancient days," says my uncle to me as he helps with the chores, "we Jews were slaves unto Pharoah in Egypt. We celebrate Pesakh, because we gained our freedom, yet here I am, still a slave of my mother Rivke-Rokhel." I never know when my uncle is joking, but when I see how hard everyone is working, I think maybe he is a little bit right.

I watch how he and Zayde take off the wooden shutters, open the windows, and fill the house with sun, wind and air. I watch them sweep away the cobwebs from the corners of the walls. They let me help them take apart the beds and take them outside into the street, where they are washed with boiling water to get rid of the bed bugs. Avrom-Layb tells me that we have bed bugs because we sleep on straw mattresses. In winter, when the house is warm and the outside is cold, bed bugs love to live in those mattresses and use our blood for food. They bite us just like mosquitoes do, so we have to kill them.

Then the walls of the house are whitewashed, the floors scrubbed to a light bright color and dusted with a yellow sand that makes them shiny and smooth. I am allowed to spill the sand on the floors when my aunts and my uncle polish them. It's great fun!

The next day, I go with my aunts to take the metal pots and pans to the center of town, where there are huge cauldrons of boiling water to make them kosher for Pesakh, but not before they are scoured with clean sand.

The day after that, the everyday dishes are put away, and the Pesakh ones taken down from their dusty place in the attic. All the wine glasses are taken out of their little boxes, including mine, which is a little blue crystal one, and of course Eliyahu Ha Navi's—that's Elijah the Prophet's Hebrew name. His elegant silver cup is polished to glow like a mirror.

I ask my aunts Shoske and Faygl if they think Elijah the Prophet will really come to our house when we open the door for him to come in during the Seder, but they only smile and shrug their shoulders. Avrom-Layb, however, tells me that there is no doubt that he will come some day to announce the coming of a better world, even if we don't know when.

"We may not even recognize him, because many times he comes in disguise when we really need him to help us. So," says my uncle, "you better be good, because you never know when he may come. It can even be this Pesakh." And my uncle smiles a big smile.

All kinds of things that are not allowed on Pesakh are packed away and stored. The new clothes ordered for the holiday are picked up. The embroidered tablecloth my aunts have worked on all through the winter is finished and made ready to be put on the table for the Seder. Kosher flour for Pesakh has been bought for baking our matzos. My mother and my bubbe have arranged a time at Berel the baker's shop for our family to bake them there. This year, I go to the bakery with them to help with the baking. My bubbe lets me make the stippled lines in the matzos with a pointed wheel.

"*Es iz shoyn tzeit*, it's about time," says my mother, "that you ask the *fier kashes*, the four questions, at the Seder by yourself without help from anyone."

"But I'm only seven years old, and I can't remember them from one year to the other," I say. But my mother pays no attention to me.

"And while we're at it," she says, "you better not drink any wine this year. *Es iz shoyn tzeit*, it's about time, you didn't fall asleep at the table and have to be put to bed in the middle of the Seder, just like a baby."

"Well," says my Uncle Avrom-Layb, coming to my rescue. "*Es iz shoyn tzeit*, it's about time, to stop all these 'about times.' I personally guarantee that Raizele will not fall asleep at the Seder table this year. You can count on it!"

My uncle is always on my side. He is seventeen years old, and I told him that when I am seventeen, I will marry him. He told me he will wait for me, but I have to hurry. He is always joking.

How fast the days go when there is so much to do! My zayde takes me with him for the first time to his Gentile neighbor to sell the *khometz*, the last of the non-Passover food. That's the custom. First we go from one corner of the house to the other with a feather, a candle and a spoon. Zayde holds the lit candle, and I help him search for the last crumb of bread with the feather, which I use to sweep anything left behind into the spoon. Then he puts all the sweepings into a little bag and we go to Yanek our neighbor, who gives us a *kopek*, a penny, for it. After Passover, Zayde will take the little bag back and give Yanek back his penny.

Finally, Passover has arrived. All has been made ready. The whole family is in the synagogue except my Aunt Liebe and I, who were left behind to watch the cooking. Actually, Liebe watches the boiling chicken soup with the *kneidlach*, matzo balls, and I watch Liebe watching.

This year I help set the holiday table with all the ritual foods for the ceremony: wine, the Paschal lamb, unleavened cakes—that's the matzo—bitter herbs, *charoset*, which is made from nuts, apples, honey and wine. Mmm, is that good!

It is quiet in the house. I watch the candles my bubbe has lit making all kinds of shadows on the wall, the windowpanes, and even on the wine bottle standing on the table. How beautiful everything looks!

Then I hear them; everyone is coming home. They're at the door. "*Gut yontev*, happy holiday, *gut Pesakh*, happy Passover," says everyone to us and to each other. I have a little towel ready for them as they wash their hands and whisper the blessing said when washing.

My bubbe takes off her hat and puts a beautiful white lace shawl over her head, and the Seder is about to begin.

"For lo, the winter has passed, the rain is over and gone, the flowers appear on the earth," everyone says together. The Seder proceeds according to its order. I have asked the four questions without a hitch. I feel very proud. Everyone smiles at me, especially Avrom-Layb, who gives me a merry wink. I feel very happy. I asked the questions in Yiddish; my uncle then asked them in Hebrew. Why is this night different than all others; why do we eat bitter herbs on this night; why do we dip two times; why on this night do we sit reclined?

"*Avodim hayinu*, for we were slaves unto Pharoah in Egypt. And had we not gone out of Egypt, we and our children's children would still be slaves unto Pharoah," everyone chants in answer.

I sit at the table with everyone. I have not had any wine, only a lick on my tongue from the three glasses needed for the blessings. The Haggada is being read in *lashon ha kodesh*, the holy language, Hebrew. I don't understand a word of it. It goes on and on. I feel my eyes closing. I try very hard to keep them open. I look to Avrom-Layb for help, but he is busy reciting the Haggada. Too late—I have fallen asleep sitting up, and I'm dreaming. But even in my dream, I am still trying to keep awake. In my dream, I look to see if my mother sees me sleeping, but my mother isn't there! In her place sits a stranger with a long, white beard. I don't know if he is smiling or frowning.

"Do you want to go to sleep now, dear little girl?" the dream creature says from one side of its smiling mouth. "It's so nice to sleep."

But the other side curls itself into an angry shout. "Don't you dare fall asleep! You want to be grown up, don't you?" Then the stranger starts to laugh.

The laughter wakes me up a little. Still half-asleep, I look to my zayde for help. I see him get up from his chair. He is holding the Haggada in one hand and is reaching for the wine with the other.

He pours the wine into Elijah's silver goblet and says, "Now let us fill the cup of Elijah with wine and open our door to him." The door is being opened, and a gust of cold air enters the room. It clears my head for the moment and, as I look at the door, suddenly something large and white bounces into the room, waving its arms about wildly. I quickly look back to my mother's seat. The stranger is no longer there, but my mother is. She is sitting with her mouth wide open, staring at this wild creature jumping about the room.

Everyone starts screaming, especially me. I don't know what is happening. Am I awake or asleep? Is this happening in a dream, or had Eliyahu HaNavi, the Prophet Elijah, really come into our house? But why is he dressed in a white sheet, and why is he jumping around so? Is it really him, or is it the stranger who was sitting in my mother's chair?

I scream and scream. I don't stop screaming even after my uncle Avrom-Layb throws off the white sheet he had covered himself with. I don't stop screaming even after he tells me over and over again that it was nobody else but him playing a joke. I don't stop screaming even after everyone hugs me and tries to comfort me. I keep sobbing as my zayde scolds my uncle for acting like a clown, disrupting the Seder and shaming the family in the sight of God.

"It's a scandal," says my zayde to Avrom-Layb, "that a man of your age should behave like such a fool."

Zayde raps on the table. "It's Pesakh; stop all this nonsense!" he says. Everyone quiets down, and the Seder continues with the reading of the Haggada.

I feel terrible, having seen how much my uncle is upset by what Zayde said. But when I sneak a peek at my uncle, a smile comes into his eyes, and he winks at me. At first I don't understand. Then I slowly realize that he did the whole thing for me, to keep me awake. And I stop sobbing and wink back at him.

Riding with the Moon

I don't tell this story very often, because I can't take the ending, when I think of Zisl. The last time I told it was about the year 2000, and then only to a small group of thirty or forty people. And sure enough, I started to cry. –*RBP*

My Aunt Fagyl was not one of my favorite people. She was the prettiest of all my mother's sisters, proud, stubborn, definitely snippy, and not at all interested in entertaining me, a little girl who was used to a lot of attention.

My father had gone to America, and my mother and I lived alone in our own small apartment in a little house in a Jewish shtetl, the small village in White Russia where I was born. We were waiting for my father to become an American citizen, so he could send for us to join him.

I, somehow, always found myself in my maternal grandparents' house among three young aunts and one uncle. It was a lively household, usually filled with talk, laughter, and the comings and goings of the many friends of my aunts and uncle.

My mother was very involved with her family inasmuch as she was the oldest. She was in many ways a second mother to her sisters and brother, and a right hand to her mother and father. She spent most of her time doing things for them, attending to all kinds of important business, which sometimes took her away for a few days. I had an ample supply of babysitters who stayed with me in our small apartment, not far from my grandparents' home, who overindulged me and kept me in a continued state of excitement.

Not, however, my Aunt Faygl. She was not at all thrilled about taking care of me. She was busy with herself, her own friends, and the chores she had to do, and she had no patience for me.

I was, therefore, not at all pleased when she insisted that she wanted to stay with me when my mother had to take my grandfather to another town where they had a hospital, because he had gotten sick. I wanted my Aunt Shoshke, who used to tell me the most wonderful stories, to stay with me, but Faygl insisted. She said she would also tell me stories and play games with me and even take me for some great walks, so I reluctantly agreed.

Faygl really tried to be nice to me, but she was very strict. She made me go to bed much earlier than even my mother did. And though she read me a story when I went to bed, it didn't sound as good as when my other aunts and uncle read to me, because she seemed to be in such a hurry. When she finished reading, she closed the door of the bedroom, and I had to go to sleep by myself in the dark.

One night, just as I was falling asleep, I thought I heard voices and other kinds of strange noises in the other room. So I got out of bed and quietly opened the door, just a crack, to see what was going on. Imagine my surprise when I saw my Aunt Faygl with a young man, whose name was Srolke, hugging and kissing.

I knew that that wasn't right, because young girls were not allowed to kiss young men or be alone with them when no one was around. I knew my grandfather and grandmother, and even my mother, would be angry if they found out. So I quietly closed the door and went back to bed smiling, because now I had a secret.

Having a secret is no fun if you can't share it with someone. So the next day, I told my cousin Zisl, who lived next door to us. Zisl was my best and worst friend. Zisl and I always played together, but we were always fighting with each other. That was because Zisl always had so many ideas of what we should do, and sometimes I didn't want to do them.

Well, Zisl was very surprised when I told her what I had seen. She also knew the rule about kissing boys. She asked me if Faygl or Srolke had seen me, and if I was going to tell anyone about it. I said they hadn't, and I wasn't. But I did wish that Faygl wouldn't make me go to bed so early.

Then a peculiar gleam came into Zisl's eyes. She clapped her hands and jumped around with excitement.

"I've got a great idea," she said. "Not only can you get Faygl not to make you go to sleep so early, but you can get something much better."

"What, what?" I asked breathlessly.

"A ride in Srolke's sleigh," declared Zisel. "He's the only one we know who has a sleigh. But you have to take me along, too. Otherwise," says my cousin in her usual bossy manner, "otherwise, I'm going to tell everyone about what your aunt was doing."

Wow! Now I was really in a pickle, because I knew that Zisl could do just that. How was I going to get my aunt's boyfriend to harness his horse and sleigh just to take Zisl and me for a ride?

"How do I ask him?" I said, feeling pretty awful by this time and sorry that I had ever told anything to Zisl.

"Nothing to it," she says. "The next time you see him, just tell him what you saw and tell him you'll tell if he doesn't take you. My brothers always get what they want by doing just that." Poor Zisl, she had three older brothers who were always bossing her around and threatening her.

I was pretty miserable the rest of the day, because I couldn't figure out how and when I was going to get the opportunity to ask Srolke for this daring request. I also pictured what my Aunt Faygl would say and do about it.

I didn't have to wait long, because my mother had not yet come home, and Faygl was still taking care of me. So that night, I was unusually agreeable about going to bed so early. And anyway, there was a big snowstorm raging outside, and the house was very cold. I was determined not to fall asleep, just in case Srolke came to see my aunt again. Sure enough, not much later, I heard my aunt greet him affectionately, and in no time at all, there were those strange sounds.

This time, I opened the door real wide and stood there staring at them. My aunt jumped up, scolding me for getting out of bed. But Srolke stopped her and spoke to me in a very affectionate tone.

"Raizelle," he said, "no one has to know I was here. Let this be a secret between the three of us. If you act like a big girl and say nothing, I'll bring a whole bag of candy just for you."

"I don't want candy," I said with a great deal of assurance. "I want you to take me for a ride with your horse and sleigh. There's lots of snow now, and pretty soon we will be going to America, and my mother said they don't have horses and sleighs with bells on them there."

My aunt and Srolke looked at each other as if they couldn't believe what they were hearing. My ready answer surprised them. My aunt started to say something, but Srolke stopped her.

"Of course," said Srolke, "of course." And he promised he would do just that, if I went back to bed and held my tongue, which I did.

My mother came home, and life took on its familiar pattern. Somehow the whole incident slipped from my mind, because there was a lot of excitement in the family. Faygl and Srolke announced that they wanted to be married, and my grandfather and grandmother agreed to the match, even though they hadn't had a matchmaker arrange the whole thing between the two families. My grandfather, however, grumbled about the outrageous behavior of modern children.

Then, one cold night a few weeks later, quite late, there was a knock on our door, and in walked Faygl and Srolke, all bundled up in their warmest clothes, their faces red from the cold. They tell my mother to help me get dressed again, as I was just about ready to go to bed.

"Come on," says Srolke with a big grin on his face. "I've come to give you a ride in my sleigh, the one with the horse and bells. Remember the bargain we made?" he says, laughing a big belly laugh. My mother doesn't know what is going on, but my aunt joins in the laughter.

"Come," she says to my mother. "This will be the last winter before you go to America. It's a beautiful night with a full moon. Come for a sleigh ride."

My mother can't resist the high spirits of my aunt and soon-to-be uncle. I am now being plied with sweaters, hats, shawls, gloves, boots. I can hardly move, I have so much clothing on. And outside we go into the cold moonlit night.

It is a white world, completely snow-covered, with a full moon hanging in a surprisingly bright blue sky. The little houses all around us look like so many snowy mounds, with tiny twinkling lights coming from their small glass windows. Icicles hanging from exposed boards glitter in the moonlight, and the stars seem like so many silver dots. The horse, sleigh and driver stand waiting silently in front of our house. A frosty hush has enveloped the night with only the crisp crackle of our footsteps on the frozen snow to break the stillness.

I stop midway to the sleigh. I have just remembered my promise to Zisl. I turn to Srolke to tell him that we must knock on Zisl's door because we have to take her with us, when all of a sudden, I hear a blood-curdling wail, then another and another, and then a whole chorus of these same sounds.

I turn to where the cries are coming from and see a cluster of large white forms completely covered in white prayer shawls, bobbing up and own in the moonlight.

"Ghosts and demons!" I scream with dread and fright. Ghosts and demons and goblins are standing in front of the synagogue, wailing at the moon. I join the wails with my own hysterical cries.

"*Narrele*, foolish one," says my mother as she grabs me in her arms. "Little foolish one, it's Rosh Chodesh Adar, the first day of the new month. Those are not ghosts or demons or goblins. They are pious, devout Jews saying the blessing for the new moon. Come, come into the sleigh, and as we ride along, I will tell you what the blessing says."

With that, my mother and aunt put me between the two of them for warmth and cover all three of us with a large fur blanket. Srolke and the driver sit up front. The driver pulls on the reins, and the horse and sleigh start their glorious gliding on the hard-packed snow.

I'm still sobbing, but the rhythm of the sleigh, the soft jingle of the sleigh bells, and my mother's voice reciting the blessing calm me.

"Praise the Lord," says my mother. "Praise the Lord from the heavens, praise Him in the heights. Praise Him and all His hosts and angels. Praise Him, sun and moon and all you stars of light. Praise Him, highest heaven and waters that are above the heavens, for He commanded, and they were created. He fixed them fast forever and ever. He gave a law which none transgresses. He ordered the moon to renew itself as a glorious crown over those He sustains from birth, who likewise will be regenerated in the future and will worship their Creator for His glorious majesty. Blessed art thou, oh Lord, who renews the months."

I watch the moon ride with us. I see the twinkling stars dance along, keeping time to the ringing of the sleigh bells. I am now warm and quiet, and as we glide along, I suddenly feel the sleigh start to rise up. Up, up we fly straight for the moon. I catch my breath. I can't believe this is really happening. I am scared and excited. Imagine flying straight up to the moon. Then without warning, we land right up there. There on the moon.

I look around and see the moon all covered with snow. No house, no trees, nothing, only snow.

Now I know why the moon is so white in the winter; it's because of the snow. I want to get out, I say, and walk on the moon.

"No," says my mother, "it's too cold." As we argue about my going, I suddenly hear a voice calling. It's calling me.

"Raizelle," it says, "Raizelle, come and get me out, come quickly!"

"It's Zisl!"I cry, "Zisl is up here on the moon! I must go to her!"

"No," says my mother. "No!"

But I tear myself out of her grip and start running towards the voice. I run and glide on the icy snow. It feels like the lake near our house when it is frozen. I glide ever faster and faster, with the wind in my face. Then I see her, my cousin Zisl. She is enclosed in a round cage of ice, with icicle bars completely shutting her in.

"Help me out of here!" cries Zisl. "Please!"

"How can I break the icicle bars?" I cry in anguish.

"With your hands!" Zisl shrieks. "Use your hands!"

I try, but the bars are so strong, so cold. I try kicking them with my feet. I bite them. I claw at them, but they won't budge. My hands are bleeding. I see the red drops of blood sinking into the white snow, making a kind of pink flower.

"Zisl," I sob, "I'll get you out. I won't leave until I do. I'll never leave you, never!"

And then I feel my mother shaking me. "Raizelle," I hear her saying again and again. "Raizelle, wake up! You fell asleep, and you started crying in your sleep! Were you dreaming?"

"Zisl," I sob, "Zisl is up there on the moon imprisoned in a house of ice. We must get her out!"

My mother and aunt start to laugh. "No," they say, "Zisl is home in her bed, fast asleep."

"But we didn't take her with us on the sleigh ride! It was her idea about the sleigh ride, and I didn't even take her with me."

My mother doesn't know what I am talking about, but she and my Aunt Faygl and Srolke assure me that the next time we go sleigh-riding, we will definitely take Zisl with us.

We never did, because lots of things happened, and we didn't go for another sleigh ride that winter. In the spring, my mother and I left for America to join my father.

Zisl's cries, however, never left me. I heard them many times, for many years, in many a dream, knowing that Zisl and all the other members of my family were no longer there. All are gone, destroyed in the Holocaust, and I am left with this strange feeling of failure.

My Grandmother Shaine Never Liked Me

When I first arrived in America from Europe, everybody made a fuss over me. One day, my cousin Dotty said, in a disgusted tone, "Everybody likes you."

I looked at her and said, "Not everybody. Bubbe Shaine never liked me. She chose you ahead of me, even though she didn't even know you!"

Dotty wasn't very impressed. She just laughed.
—RBP

My paternal grandmother Shaine Kolner never liked me. I once asked her to name her favorite grandchildren, and she put me at the end of a list of seventeen. It made me feel real bad. So I asked her right out, "Bubbe, why don't you like me?"

She answered me without any hesitation: "*Vile du bist a shtik foon dien mamme.* Because you are just like your mother."

"What's wrong with my mother? I said, putting my hands on my hips, my legs spread apart. I was ready to defend my mother with my life.

"Aw! Aw!" said my grandmother, gloatingly, pointing a finger at me. "You see, just like your mother."

This remark was more than I could bear. I swallowed hard, fighting to hold back my tears. "Why don't you like my mother?" I murmured, trying to hide my humiliation.

My grandmother's face softened, and in a somewhat kinder voice she spoke to me, as you might say, "man to man." "*Zi blawts zikh.*" Literally, this means, she blows herself up, but in plain *mammeloshn*, it mean's she's conceited. "*Zi dainkt as zi iz dos shertzl foon teple*—she thinks she is the lid of the pot. " In other words, the cat's meow.

To tell you the truth, I didn't know what my grandmother was driving at, but I kept quiet.

"Just because," said my grandmother, "she had a pretty face and knew a few chapters of Toyre, your fool of a father took her without a cent of *naden*, dowry." My grandmother lowered her eyes. "People thought it was a big joke. I was ashamed to lift my head up in town. Imagine, a boy like him, so popular, so lively, a good earner—taking a stuck-up with no money!" Here my grandmother sighed with deep emotion.

"And to make matters worse," she continued, "now that he went to America and is sending her money and other things, she hardly even talks to me. I hear—I hear what goes on in her apartment. Night and day people coming, going, laughing, singing—I hear," my grandmother said sadly. "You think she would invite me in sometimes when they read the *Forvertz* (*The Jewish Daily Forward*) that he sends her from America. I would also like to hear what is going on in America, but no, all I hear through the wall is the laughing and the carousing."

Here I have to explain that my mother and I lived in my paternal grandfather's house, which had been divided into three separate apartments at his death. What had once been a more or less comfortable dwelling was now a cramped living space for three separate households. My Uncle Borakh, my father's brother, lived in the largest one with his wife and six children. They had two bedrooms and a large kitchen, in which there was never an inch of space. My mother and I lived in the middle, one bedroom with a medium-sized kitchen. My grandmother Shaine lived on the other side of us in a small bedroom and an equally small kitchen. We shared a common wall with both my uncle and grandmother.

The wall we shared with my grandmother was that of the kitchen, which also served as living room and dining room. All activities took place there. My grandmother heard all that went on in our house simply by lying on her bed. That is, she would have liked to have heard all that was going on, but all she really heard were muffled voices.

Sadly, my grandmother continued her litany in a voice that would have melted a stone. "When your father was here, he used to come in sometimes and make me laugh. He would sing me a little song, tell me a joke, talk about this and that—but now I'm lonely like a dog."

I felt terrible. I missed my father, too. I came home to my mother ready to do battle for my poor, neglected grandmother.

I confronted my mother with all her transgressions. Why are you conceited? Why didn't you give my father *naden*? Why don't you invite Bubbe Shaine in to hear the news about America from the *Forvertz*?

My mother was thunderstruck. "That *makhishaife!*" she said. "That witch! Imagine filling a child's head with such exaggerations, such lies! I never want you to speak to her again, do you hear?

"Imagine," continued my mother, unable to contain herself, "imagine her saying that she's lonely! She has three other children living right here next to her with seventeen grandchildren, and she's always running around sticking her nose into everyone's business. That's Zavelikhe for you." My mother meant that as a put-down. You see, my grandfather's name was Zavel, and if you wanted to demean his wife, you called her Zavelikhe.

"That's Zavelikhe," my mother said with great disdain, "going to every wedding in town, invited or not. Peering in through every window if she can't come in through the door."

The image of my grandmother peering in through the window all alone at a stranger's wedding caught my imagination. I could not get it out of my mind. I felt sorry for my grandmother despite my mother's outraged defense. I kept thinking about it whenever I looked at the wall that united and divided us from her.

One day, as I was sitting at the table, I noticed a crack in that wall, starting at the top of our leather sofa. Going over to examine it, I traced its descent to the floor. It was deeply etched into the plaster.

We were due to leave for America to join my father that year, and my mother was not about to fix anything. Quarrels had already broken out among my uncle, my aunt and my grandmother as to who would take over our apartment. My mother was having none of this. "Let those dogs fight over it themselves, " she would say, holding her aristocratic nose in the air.

Well, as I was studying the crack in the wall, it suddenly occurred to me that I could perhaps make my grandmother like me a little better. I would show her that I was not like my mother. So everyday, when my mother was not around, I opened the crack in the wall a little wider with a sharp stone. When I got to the wooden slats that held the plaster together, I started to work on an opening on my grandmother's side of the wall. Little by little, the hole in my grandmother's wall took shape, and when I put my eye to it, I could look straight into my grandmother's home.

There, I thought, all my grandmother had to do was put her ear to the wall, and she would be able to hear all the news about America from the *Forvertz.* I was very satisfied with the job I had done. The only thing left to do now was to tell her.

I had, however, neglected to clean up the plaster that now lay on the floor behind the sofa. My mother, noticing a white, powdery cloud floating around the sofa every time the door opened, moved the sofa away and found the hole.

When she found out that it was my doing, I received such a spanking that I still remember it today. I was not able to sit down for a week. Even worse was the humiliating letter she wrote to my father about how impossible I was to control, and how I was always getting into all kinds of mischief. She wrote that she was sure that I took after his side of the family, that I was a *shtick foon* my Bubbe Zavelikhe. I never got to tell my grandmother what I had tried to do, either, because my mother plastered the wall back to its original state.

Several weeks after we arrived in America, my father took me for a walk to acquaint me with the neighborhood. He took my hand and walked me right into the candy store that was on the corner of our street. He bought me a chocolate ice cream soda, which he wanted me to drink through a straw. I had never seen a straw before. After teaching me how to use it, he sat looking at my struggle to live up to his expectations.

Suddenly, his eyes filled with tears, and he said in a voice that seemed to have developed a fog in it, "Raizelle, Raizelle, I want to thank you for trying to take care of my mother." And my father, grabbing me in his arms, began to cry.

The Strike in the Tannery

In researching this story, I came across the Tanners Union Manifesto, from 1900 to 1907, that was the basis for the strike. Here is the translation: Our Bund (union) does not originate in the imagination, it is not the brainstorm of a few hotheads, but is a natural, necessary product of everyday life. It is a mighty weapon forged and sharpened through constant fiery struggle. Storms and hurricanes are its godfather; solidarity and awareness have swaddled it; sweat and blood have nursed it; prisons in Siberia raised it; celebration and sorrow, triumph and defeat have given it strength; soldiers, Cossacks and police have celebrated its Bar Mitzvah!
-RBP

When I first started telling stories, my focus was my childhood in the shtetl, the small town where I was born. I felt it was my duty to keep alive, if only in story, the memory of my family and the people of my town, who were wiped out during the great disaster of the Holocaust.

Since my own remembrances were that of a child of seven, I enlisted my mother's help to fill in and authenticate my own recall. I questioned her about everything. I would go to her house and stay several hours every week. My mother loved those sessions, as they kept me with her for an extended period of time, and because they also triggered her own memories.

We were almost at the end of our interviews when I told her I had only two more topics I wanted to cover. "Crime," I say. "Was there any crime in the shtetl?"

"No," says my mother.

"Come on, Ma," I say. "There must have been *some* crime."

"Not really," says my mother. "Everyone was so poor, what was there to steal? Maybe some time a *shpikhler*, a pantry or root cellar, would be broken into. They would steal special kinds of food, like jam, or *vishnick*, homemade cherry brandy. Really, nothing to speak of."

"It seems to me Papa once told me about a man who lived on a farm on the outskirts of town. He sold horses. He had his head cut off. What about that?"

"Oh yes," says my mother, "I heard of that, too, but I didn't pay much attention to it." After an answer like that, I decided I might as well go to the next question.

"How about prostitution? Was there prostitution in the shtetl?"

"No!" says my mother.

"What do you mean 'no'! I'm sure there must have been a girl or two of easy virtue to whom the boys came to visit. I'm sure men were no different in the shtetl than they are in any other place in the world."

"Well," says my mother grudgingly, "there was one girl, but she was a very nice girl, very poor. She came from a very poor family."

"You knew her?"

"I went to school with her brother. The family was very poor. The boys used to bring her food, maybe some money. She gave it all to the family."

"Who were they?" I wanted to know. "What was their name?"

"I'm not telling!" says my mother defiantly.

"Oh come on, Ma, I won't tell anyone."

"No, no one, only the whole world." And she didn't tell me!

"Well, Ma, now we are finished." I say, very self-satisfied.

"Oh we *are*, are we?" says my mother. "So you think we're finished, my educated daughter, my *farbrente Socialistke*, my red-hot Socialist. You asked me about everything, so how come you never asked me about strikes, protests, and unions in the shtetl? After all, there was *eppes*, some kind of a revolution brewing in Russia. After all, Wysokie was on the railroad line which connected it to all the important cities like Brest, Minsk, Bialystock, Warsaw, even Vilna, and it wasn't hard for these young revolutionaries to get to us. Then, of course, we had plenty of our own.

"I don't know if you remember, you were only a child about six years old, but one day we went to the marketplace just as they were leading a group of political prisoners out of jail in order to send them some other place, heaven knows where, and they were all bound in chains. Nobody wanted to look at them or be associated with them, as the Polish police were very hard on revolutionary sympathizers. But you recognized your Uncle Srolke's brother, and before I could stop you, you called out in a voice that the whole town could hear, 'Look, Mama, look, there goes Itzik, and look, he is full of chains!'

"In fact, my own father, your grandfather, went on strike with the tanners when I was a little girl. In fact, we had a meeting in our house."

I was flabbergasted! My conservative, religious Zayde, my grandfather, was active in a strike! I had never heard anyone mention this topic.

"Look, Ma," I said, "Next week we'll spend a lot of time on that subject. Till then, see if you can remember some of the details of what your mother told you. You know me, I like details." My mother smiled; she was satisfied. And she now had me back again just where she wanted, in her house for several hours.

The very next day, I went to the public library to see if I could get some information on the subject of labor unrest in that time and place. There was none to be found. I wanted to make sure of my mother's information. And so I went to YIVO, the Jewish Research Institute, which is an archive for Jewish Eastern Europe. The librarian said she had nothing in English, but she did have a Yiddish book on this very topic written by Sophie Dubnov Ehrlich, the daughter of Simon Dubnov, who was the most famous Yiddish historian of that time. If I could read Yiddish, she would let me have the book only to be used in the library. The book was old, and in poor condition, on the verge of falling apart.

And so every day for a whole month, I sat in the library at YIVO, struggling with this old Yiddish book. But it was worth it. I found much information in it.

What my mother said was true. There were many strikes in that area in the years between the turn of the century and the First World War. In fact, our little town of Wysokie-Litewsk was mentioned by name as one of the *shtetlakh* having a strike in its one leather factory. At that time, even in the small villages, they were beginning to realize that a worker did not have to work fifteen, sixteen hours a day to earn a living. That a human being had some kind of rights, that even the very poor, if they got together, could change things.

"This happened when I was seven years old, " says my mother next time I see her, and her eyes take on an excited gleam almost bordering on delight. "I remember it clearly. It was just after Pesakh, when my father and all the tanners at the *gabarneh*, the tannery, went out on strike. The leatherworks was the largest factory in town. In fact, my father had come to Wysokie from the town of Drogachine to work there. He worked in the section where they polished the leather and then stamped out the soles for making boots. As a child, I used to hear my parents talk about how rich Reb Fievel Rosenfeld had gotten because leather was in such demand. This was because the peasants were all starting to wear leather boots instead of those *shmattes* they used to wear around their feet to keep warm.

"It was very hard working in the terrible factories of those days. Old, dirty, smelly, crowded, without air, without sanitation. And the machines they used were so clumsy, so unsafe, that accidents happened everyday.

"Don't think that only the Jewish workers had it hard. The peasants, both Russian and Polish, who left their land to work there had it even harder. They worked in the wet part of the leatherworks, where they soaked the hides in chemicals in order to clean and soften them. Not only were they paid less, but the place smelled like you shouldn't know from it. It smelled worse than a toilet. It got into their hair, their skin, their breath. You could smell them coming from a mile away.

"But the Jews had another problem that the *goyim* didn't have. In order to keep the Shabbes, they had to work all Saturday night and a half a day Sunday, too.

"You know the very religious men in the shtetl were against the strike. They said that you shouldn't bite the hand that feeds you. And they said that it was more important to study Toyre than start all this trouble. Yet even they saw how not right it was."

"How do you know all this?" I asked my mother.

"Of course I didn't know all this myself. What I'm telling you I heard from my mother and father and from my own teacher, who, if you ask me, was a *bissl*, a little bit, of a revolutionary himself.

"This is how it all started. It happened one Friday that a stranger came into town. No one knew anything about him because he didn't go to Reb Dovidle Nachman's Inn to stay, and he didn't come into the synagogue for the Shabbes prayers. Also, he had a queer look to him, sort of worn-out, pale, with burning black eyes. He came into town and disappeared. So Saturday, after *cholent*, the traditional Sabbath stew, the young people of the town who were milling around in the street were filled with excitement. They seemed to know that this person was someone special. They were exchanging knowing glances with one another. By the next morning, the entire shtetl knew that the young stranger was no buyer of leather, no trader, but one of those revolutionaries from Bialystock. He had been sent by the Jewish Labor Bund to explain to the workers from the tannery how to make a union. Up to this time, no one in town had taken on this responsibility, although there was plenty of grumbling and complaining.

"This turn of events inspired the young hotheads to start singing their revolutionary songs as they marched past the synagogue. So far all they did was sing. They sang all the time, songs of labor, poverty, revolt, songs of making a better world. But as the day wore on, there were whispers that a meeting was going to be held that night behind the old cemetery grounds. The young stranger from Bialystock would be there, and also Layzer Ber, the baker's son, who was the fastest and best paid worker in the tannery. Everyone looked up to him. He was going to introduce the young man.

"My father didn't want to go to the meeting. He told this to my mother, who was much more ready to join the agitators. My father was a nice, gentle person, very religious, and not one for making trouble. But my mother, she was the fiery one, and she told my father that if he didn't go, she would go alone.

"I was only a little girl," says my mother, "but I remember the argument my mother and father had. I remember my mother saying, 'Mortkhe, something has to be done. You can't go on working like a *hazel*, a donkey. You're falling away from tiredness. Besides, what you earn isn't enough to live on. You know that yourself. There must be a strike, because Reb Fievel Rosenfeld will never pay more or change the working hours. He is getting fat on other people's sweat and blood. And his wife, Printze the *pristeh,* the grand lady, goes around with her double chin and her gold earrings, holding her nose in the air. Why should he pay more if he is not forced to do it? And this working all night on Saturday to make up for keeping the Shabbes is a *shandeh un a kharpeh,* a shame and a disgrace! Isn't he himself a Jew? How could he do this to his own people?'

"My father had no answer to this, and anyway, my mother won most of the arguments. My father never wanted to make fights, so they both went that night to the meeting in the back of the cemetery, along with most of the older men who were the tanners, and, of course, all the young men of the town.

"First Layzer Ber stood up, his face flushed, his eyes sparkling like two Shabbes candles. He took our a sheet of paper and started to talk to the people. He told them about the stranger, a union organizer sent down from the Jewish Labor Bund in Bialystock to help form a union. Not only for the Jews, but also for the Gentiles. It was very important they they also join the union.

Everyone started talking, saying that the peasants would never join. The church told them not to go against their bosses, and also to stay away from the Jews, who were nothing but troublemakers. But Layzer Ber said that they must get them to join, otherwise they couldn't win. This was an unheard of thing, to work together with the goyim. A riot almost started, because everyone started talking and shouting at the same time. They said the peasants couldn't be trusted, that at the first sign of anything going wrong, they would blame the Jews and pogroms would start, and the Jews once again would be beaten and, God forbid, killed.

"But the young man from Bialystock held up his hand and shouted through some kind of speaking horn. Then everybody quieted down. In a loud voice, he made a speech, saying that the Gentiles were workers, too, that they too had to be taught that all men were brothers, that both Jewish and Gentile workers had one enemy, the Bosses, and if they get together, they could help themselves and each other and make a better world for everyone. Then he ended with, 'Down with the capitalists, long live the working class!'

"Then Layzer Ber recited the Manifesto of the Union, and the whole crowd caught up the cry and burst into shouts of Hurrah! Hurrah! Everyone was very inspired, and they all marched back to town singing.

"My mother knew all the revolutionary songs," says my mother. "Oy, she had such a lovely voice, and I can't sing a note! Well, anyway, after that, there were many meetings, even one in our house. The Russian police were always dragging somebody off to prison, and Reb Fievel Rosenfeld had special guards with dogs watching the factory. That was before the strike started. I used to have to go to bring my father his lunch, and I was so much afraid of those dogs.

"Then all the men went out on strike after Pesakh, even the peasants. Oy, was everyone scared! But not the young hotheads; they weren't scared.

"One night, the church bells started to ring like there was a fire in the town. Everyone woke up and ran into the street. We couldn't see any fire, so everyone started running to the church to see why the bells were ringing. And what do you think they saw? Some of those red-hot Socialists had, during the night, climbed up that tall church steeple and hung a big red flag on it. They caught those young men, two Jews and three goyim, who did this together.

"After that there were lots of arrests, but it didn't stop the strike. Then the shoemakers and the tailors also went on strike for a few days. It took a few weeks, and the workers won.

"They won a lot of benefits; more pay, better hours, no Saturday night work. They also asked for benefits that you and your children, my dear daughter, are still fighting for.

"So, my little bud," says my mother to me, "keep up the good work. There are still plenty of poor and hungry people around. There is still lots to be done!"

The Golden Land

A Real American Girl

My friend took her little daughter, who was six years old, to hear a Mother's Day program I was doing in which I told this story about how seasick I was on the ship crossing the ocean to America. As I say in the story, we had been told by some of my mother's friends back home that the best remedy for this was to take along a dark pumpernickel bread and a large tin of shmaltz herring. I then explained to those who did not know what shmaltz herring was and its important role in the diet of the people of Eastern Europe.

A few days later, my friend called to tell me that her little girl had developed a stomach ache and was feeling nauseous. When she tried to comfort her by telling her that she would give her some Milk of Magnesia and everything would be okay, the little girl said, "No Mommy, what I need is some shmaltz herring!"

–RBP

My mother and I arrived in America on one of the hottest days of the summer. The day was Friday, the date June 29, 1929, and the temperature was somewhere in the high 90's. It was a sad day for many Americans, because on that day the stock market had its first major crash. It was the beginning of the Great Depression.

I was seven years old and very excited about being with my father, whom I hadn't seen since I was a baby. In fact, I was only six months old when he left for America.

For me, crossing the ocean was ten days of complete and total misery. I was seasick from beginning to end. And although everyone assured me that I was not going to die from this, I knew for sure that my death was just about to happen any moment. This was happening to me in spite of all the good advice and remedies offered by the people of our town for seasickness.

"Take along some of our good, dark pumpernickel bread," they told my mother, "and take a generous tin of shmaltz herring." The herring of shmaltz herring fame is a plain little fish that is preserved in salt and oil and eaten raw. It was the main food of poor Jewish people throughout Eastern Europe, good for any kind of occasion and especially good when one needed a lift. I must tell you that it is still one of my favorite foods to this day. However, nowadays it is hard to find a store that still sells it. But during the time I was on the ship, I couldn't look another piece of herring in the face. Every time I saw my mother coming toward me with another piece, I started throwing up before she even got near me.

My mother couldn't understand why it didn't work on me; she felt just wonderful eating it. "It tastes much better than those strange things they feed us upstairs in the dining room," she said.

I spent my time moaning and groaning, feeling very sorry for myself, wishing that my father had never gone to America, had never even heard of America. If only I was back home playing with my cousin Zisl! I knew that this trip would never end; it would go on like this forever.

Then it happened! One day just before lunch we heard someone shout, "There she is, *Gut tsu danken.* Praise be to God; we have arrived in America!" I forgot about my being sick; I forgot about my nausea, and I joined my mother and all the other shouting, cheering immigrants on the deck of the ship. And there she really was, the much-loved lady of the harbor—the Statue of Liberty. People laughed and cried, kissed and hugged each other, and I along with them.

Throughout these many years, my father had worked very hard to gather enough money to send for us. He was now a citizen of America, and so he had the privilege of bringing us here. My mother was not happy leaving her family, although I'm sure she also wanted to be with my father. However, on the ship, she cried and she cried about having to leave her father, mother, sisters, brother. I, taking my cue from her, also complained bitterly about not having anyone to play with.

Well, finally the boat docked, and all the people ran off into the arms of welcoming relatives and friends—but not us. We couldn't find my father. We waited and waited until almost all the people were gone, and still no Papa!

"It's so hot!" I cried. "My stomach hurts me, I have to go to the toilet, I'm tired, I'm nauseous, and where's Papa?" I started crying. My mother had no patience for me. She was not only worried about my father, but she was by now very upset about the time.

"It's almost Shabbes, the Sabbath," said my mother. "Soon it will be time to *bench lickt*, to light the Sabbath candles, and we will still be lost somewhere here in wild America."

The immigration officials, seeing that no one had come to claim us, took us back to another smaller boat and told us we would have to wait for my father on Ellis Island, which was the place for immigrants with problems. I started to hate America right then and there.

We had just about made ourselves comfortable in one of the wire mesh cubicles when a short, fat, balding man with a red face, sweating profusely, rushed into the cubicle. On seeing us, he burst into tears. My mother seemed to know him, as she went into his outstretched arms. They both stood there weeping and holding each other. I, sitting on my stool, observed this scene with a feeling of shock and disappointment. Then my father turned toward me, looked at me lovingly with his red-rimmed eyes which now matched his face, held out his arms to me and said, "*Nu*, how do you like your Papa?"

I stared at him in disbelief and burst into tears. "Are you sure he is my Papa?" I asked my mother. "My Papa is handsome, and this man doesn't look like him."

At first my mother and father looked unbelievingly at me; then they both started laughing. "How do you know I was handsome?" asked my father, as he pulled me toward him.

"You don't look like the pictures you sent us," I answered, while being hugged and kissed by this laughing, crying little man.

"No," said my father. "Well, I'll see if I can do something about looking better, more like those pictures some other time."

You see, throughout his absence, my father had written letters to us, sent us money, and what I liked best of all, he sent us portrait pictures of himself. In fact, my mother would put me to sleep by singing me my favorite lullaby, while I held onto his picture. I used to think my mother made up that song just for me. It went something like this:

In America your Papa,
Sleep my Raizele,
You're a dear child.
In the meanwhile,
Sleep now, sleep, lu lu.

He will send us twenty dollars
And his picture, too.
And he'll send for us, God bless him,
There we'll live anew.

Actually, I later found out it was written by Sholom Aleichem, the great Jewish writer.

The father of my pictures was always dressed in a double-breasted, pin-striped suit with a fedora felt-trimmed hat, spats on his shoes, gloves in one hand and a cane in the other. To top it all off, he wore dark, horn-rimmed glasses. He looked tall and handsome. Not at all like this father. I knew it was hot, and he couldn't wear all those clothes, but at least, I thought resentfully, he could have put on his glasses!

My father, on the other hand, was also disappointed in me. He told me this years later. The photos my mother sent to him of me were that of a pretty, blonde, curly-haired little girl with a winning smile. What he saw was a chubby seven-year-old with a boy's bob, which had been given me to make sure I would not be carrying the lice most every child had in their hair in the shtetl. My short hair was now straight, dirty blonde, no curls. My front teeth were missing, and on my face was a constant scowl.

All in all it was a poor beginning. My father, however, took it all in stride. He told us he had gotten lost on the way to the pier and had gone to some other place. However, says he, "Now we are going to go home in a taxi. No more getting lost."

In the taxi cab on the way home, he holds onto my mother with one hand and with the other, he reaches into his pocket and takes out a long yellow object. He holds it up and with a satisfied grin asks me if I know what it is. I shake my head no.

"It's a banana," he says merrily. Only he said "panana."

"In America," says my father, "all the children eat pananas. You want to try one now?" asks my father with a definite plea in his voice. "It's very tasty."

I felt I had already done enough damage to our relationship, and I wanted to please him. After all, no matter how disappointed I was, it seemed he was my real father. I took the banana.

"First," says my father, "You have to peel it, only halfway." He shows me how. "Then you hold it with the peel hanging down like an umbrella.

"Now," says my father, "Take a bite." I take a bite. It has a strange texture that is unfamiliar to my palate. It feels squashy, gooey and cloyingly sweet. It reminds me of my nausea. I start to gag. My mother puts a handkerchief under my mouth, and I throw up.

My father takes the half-peeled banana, arranges the peel to cover the exposed half, and sadly puts it back into his pocket. Then, as if a brand-new thought has entered his head, he lifts up his hand and with a finger pointing up to heaven, he smiles with eyes twinkling.

"Someday," he says, "someday soon you'll be able to eat a whole panana, and then you'll be a real American girl!"

Actually, it's only recently that I've been able to eat them. You see, the doctor told me that at my age, I need the potassium.

Angelina's Garden

When my Italian daughter-in-law asked me to tell this story to her mother, the woman had tears in her eyes, and she said, "That was my house, and my garden. But my grandmother was very nice!" –*RBP*

Living in the Bronx, New York, on Longfellow Avenue was not the ideal place for a little girl who had recently come from a rural shtetl in White Russia. Longfellow Avenue between 173rd Street and Jennings had no trees, no grass, no flowers. It had five-story brick buildings on both sides of the street that seemed pasted together, without space for even a blade of grass to sneak in.

The shtetl was poor, but for me, a child who was loved and coddled, that had no meaning. All I knew was that I longed for the meadow with its yellow buttercups, the river and brook so near our house, the crab apple tree right outside of our window, and the gardens of both my grandmothers. There were many adjustments in my life that were more meaningful, but this drastic change in my environment made me cry every time I thought of my old home.

Being the kind of child who manages to try things on her own, I started to investigate the area around my school. My father had laid out the route I was to take to Public School 66. After a few months of religiously doing what I was told, I decided there must be other ways to go. So I tried a street that went around to the back side of the school. Keeping the school building in view so I wouldn't get lost, I headed down a street called Boone Avenue, and to my delight, I saw an open lot with a large rock, grass growing around it, and a few trees growing in various places in the area.

Across the street, standing all by itself, was a little wooden house. It had a porch, it had trees and bushes, and to my great joy, it had a small garden right in front of it. I had no time to investigate my newfound treasure as the school bell had already sounded, but I knew I would be back soon, very soon.

So started my clandestine love affair with the little house and its garden. I did not tell my parents of my new route to school. It was out of the way and took longer to get there, so I had to run to get to school on time. I knew my mother would definitely object to my running, and I hadn't yet developed enough trust in my father to confide my secret in him; I knew him only a few months. And so I kept everything to myself until that fateful day a few weeks later.

One day, I somehow managed to arrive a little earlier at this heavenly place, when who do I see coming out of the house but Angelina, a girl in my class. Running to catch up to her, I plied her with questions in my broken English. "Who live there? You house, you garden?"

Angelina is a very nice girl, and she tries to understand what I am saying.

"Yes," she says, "I live there with my mother and father and my grandmother, who also doesn't speak English. The garden is hers, and she doesn't let anyone go in or touch what she grows there."

"What she speaks?" I ask her.

"Italian; we are Italian." I do not know what Italian is or how it sounds, but I say nothing, and I make up my mind to cultivate Angelina's friendship.

I try to go home with her as much as I can, even though it makes me late returning to my house. I make up a different excuse each time to tell my mother. I try to meet her going to school, even though I have to run even more to arrive at her house early. Little by little, Angelina becomes more and more friendly. I don't say anything to my parents about my new friend, because I know Angelina is not Jewish. She wears a cross around her neck. Somehow I know my parents would object to this friendship. But I don't care. I like Angelina, and I'm sure if she begins liking me, she might let me in to see her grandmother's garden.

Then one day, I take my life in my hands and pose the question. "Angelina, you thinks I come into garden just a minute?"

Angelina's eyes open wide with fright. "Oh, I can't do that! I even promised my grandmother that I would never touch anything there, and I'm sure she would become very angry if I let you in, even for a minute."

Tears fill my eyes without my even trying to make them come.

I'm really heartbroken. Angelina sees my pain. "My, do you want to go in there so much?" she asks.

So then I try to explain to her in my poor English how much I miss my old home, with its trees and flowers and my two grandmothers who always let me and my cousin Zisl play in their garden.

"They no even mind if sometimes we eats some of the lima beans ready to picking," I say.

I can see that Angelina feels sorry for me. Then, much to my delight, she lowers her voice and whispers in my ear, "I'll let you in this time, but only for one minute." I'm too thrilled to even say thank you.

She quietly opens the gate and lets me in. I see a really small garden, all arranged in little sections where different kinds of things are growing.

"What a tiny garden," I say to Angelina. "My grandmas' gardens were so much bigger than this one." And just when I want to tell her how glad I am to at least see this one, her grandmother comes out on the porch and sees us.

Angelina and I stand petrified with fear. And then her grandmother starts to scream in a language I absolutely do not understand, not even one word. Angelina pulls me out of the garden, and we both start to run. When we are some distance from the house, we stop and catch our breath. I feel very guilty for getting Angelina into trouble with her grandmother, but I am also curious what she was yelling about.

I ask Angelina what her grandmother said. "She said I can't play with you anymore because you are a dirty Jew and a Christ killer, and you will always get me to do things that I shouldn't."

"No, I won't," I say, and I run home crying.

When I got home, my father was there. He saw how upset I was, and he asked me in a kind voice what had happened. I told him about the trees and the grass and the gardens in the shtetl. I told him about Angelina and her grandmother's garden, and I told him what her grandmother said about me.

"I know I made Angelina take me into her garden, but I only wanted a look," I wailed. "Then her grandmother said I was a dirty

Jew and a Christ killer. I know I'm Jewish, but I know I'm not dirty, because Mama makes me wash all the time. And I know I'm not a killer. But who is Christ?

My father patted my hair. "You are a good girl, so don't worry about Angelina. I'm sure her grandmother will forgive her for letting you in her garden. As far as Christ is concerned, I wouldn't worry about him, either, because he was a nice Jewish boy."

My First Thanksgiving

Do you remember the movie Avalon, *directed by Barry Levinson? He said he wanted someone who came from Europe at an early age, who was not a professional actress, for the part of the mother. An agent called me and told me to come down for an audition.*

They gave me a script to read. They had a whole camera crew making a video of my audition. It was a very funny scene about the father feeding the dog under the table. Everybody laughed and clapped.

When it was over, the woman in charge came over to me. "You did a very fine job, Mrs. Perry," she said, "but I don't think you're right for the part."

Given the reaction I had gotten from the scene, I was surprised, and I asked her why.

"Unfortunately," she said, "you don't have a Jewish accent." *–RBP*

P.S. 66 in the Bronx, New York, was suddenly ablaze with color. Windows that had formally looked out on drab streets and dull five-story brick houses were now the glassy fields for falling autumn leaves. Young hands given free rein had colored them exotic shades of wine, orange, yellow, red, purple, green—and some daring artists even added black and brown.

In the middle of these messengers of autumn, other windows cradled the large round bulging shapes of pumpkins. Their facial expressions of smiles, frowns, lots of teeth, no teeth, were a complete mystery to me, an immigrant child of a small Eastern European shtetl. My mother and I had just a few short months before arrived in America to join my father, who had for six years worked to bring us over. There had never been a pumpkin in my experience of the world before, and I accepted it as I did so many other things in America, with resigned apprehension.

In our third-grade auditorium period, we learned songs about pumpkins and turkeys. We learned Halloween songs, but mostly we learned Thanksgiving hymns. I liked the hymns the best. "We gather together to ask the Lord's blessing"—to me that song sounded very Jewish. It sounded very much like the songs we sang in my old home, because we were also always praising the Lord and asking for His blessing. Only we called Him *HaShem*.

In our classroom, we talked about Halloween, about witches and goblins and scary things. I thought it was a very strange kind of holiday. Consider my horror when on Halloween morning on my way to school, I was pelted on the head with a stocking filled with flour, and on my way home, my new navy blue coat was marked up with colored chalk. My tormentors were a group of boys from my third-grade class who called out, "Greenhorn, greenhorn, trick or treat," and then added the merry salutation of "Happy Halloween!"

I came home very upset and told my mother that in America people did some very mean things. Even Harvey Handlesman, the boy who sat next to me in class and whom I liked, was one of the kids who chalked my coat. My mother didn't know what to say because she didn't understand it, either. However, when I told this to my father, he said, "Not to worry, because the chalk can be wiped off, and this in America is called having fun."

"I want to go back home," I said. "I don't like it here."

My father patted me on the head and said, "You'll change your mind someday; you'll see."

A few days later, Mrs. Holstein, my third-grade teacher, told us we were now going to learn about the Pilgrims. She told us how and why they came to America, and what they did to survive here. When I heard that the Pilgrims came from Europe, that they had a very hard time coming across on the Mayflower, because many of them were sick and afraid, I brightened up considerably. This I understood. This I could relate to. Hadn't I just come from Europe? Didn't we also come here to be free to live as Jews? And I knew that everyone was afraid; this I knew for sure.

Later, when I found out what a terribly hard time they had that first winter, how they suffered but worked together, how they made friends with the Indians and how they were always reading the Bible, I just simply fell in love with every one of them. So imagine my joy when I found out that a play about the Pilgrims was being considered by the third grade, which would be performed in the auditorium. All interested third-graders were invited to audition for the various parts. The play was to be The Courtship of Miles Standish, written by a very important writer whose name was Henry Wadsworth Longfellow.

Our teacher told us the story of the play: Captain Miles Standish was a great hero to all the people of this Pilgrim colony, because he was a very brave man and a gallant fighter. When his wife died, he was very lonely. For many years he lived alone, but he did not like it. One day, he noticed a beautiful young girl, and he liked her very much. He wanted to marry her, but he wasn't sure of himself because he was much older. He talked about this to the young man who was his helper. His name was John Alden. John Alden also liked this beautiful young girl, whose name was Priscilla. He didn't tell this to Miles Standish, because he felt if his captain wanted Priscilla, he, John Alden, had no right to want her, even if he was her age. Captain Miles Standish then told John Alden to go to Priscilla and ask her to marry him, because he could not speak as nicely as John Alden did. Well, in the end Priscilla said she did not want to marry Captain Standish. She wanted John Alden, even if the Captain would be angry.

I liked the play very much, so I asked my mother if she thought I could try out for a part.

My mother said, "Absolutely, you are a born actress. And besides, you have a lot of stage experience. You appeared in all the dramatic presentations of your nursery school in our shtetl. You were absolutely the best snowflake there."

Not being so sure of myself, I checked with my teacher Mrs. Holstein, who looked a little doubtful, but then said, "Why not?"

Something in my childish heart warned me against doing this, but the lure of the stage was too strong to resist, and I raised my hand in the auditorium when the teacher in charge, Miss Delaney, asked for volunteers. She asked each of us what part we wanted to play, and I asked for the part of Priscilla, the heroine. Miss Delaney hesitantly gave me the page with Priscilla's few precious lines. I took the text home and studied hard. My mother went over the lines with me word for word.

When it came to my turn to recite, I was one of the few children who did not have to look at my paper. My heart beat fast as I went up on stage. With my head erect, my eyes sparkling, I was determined to be the best Priscilla in the entire third grade. John Alden had now asked his famous question: Will the fair Priscilla consider the request of the outstanding Captain Miles Standish and be his bride?

I bowed my head coquettishly and answered in my most endearing manner, "Vy daunt you spick for yourself, Jaun?"

All the teachers of the entire third grade starting laughing. I stood there looking at them with astonishment. Why were they laughing? Had I done something wrong? I looked at my own teacher Mrs. Holstein, and I could see the anger in her eyes.

Miss Delaney tried not to smile as she spoke to me. "That was very good, Roslyn," she said. "You are certainly a fine actress. But I'm afraid this part is not for you. You see, the Pilgrim maid Priscilla would never have spoken with a Yiddish accent."

So that was why everyone laughed! They were laughing at me, and the humiliation cut deeply into my childish soul. Tears came to my eyes, and I ran off the stage.

Mrs. Holstein managed to get me into the chorus of the play, and we sang "We gather together to ask the Lord's blessing." However, my heart was broken, even though Mrs. Holstein assured me that someday soon, my accent would disappear and then I could become a great actress if that was what I wanted. I then and there resolved never to ask my mother to help me with anything that had to do with school, because I knew that her accent was much worse than mine. And I also resolved never ever to speak Yiddish again. I was going to become a real American girl.

Many hard years would pass before I realized that my mother knew a great many things that were very important, even though she spoke with a Yiddish accent. Many years would pass before I realized my loss in giving up Yiddish, my mother tongue. It has taken me a great deal of time and effort to reclaim it, but I did—*Ikh hob dos geton*!

A Trip to the Coca Cola Plant

I recently told this story to an elder group in Florida. When I got to the part when I said that the class was going to go to a Coca Cola plant in New York City, three women jumped up out of the audience and yelled, "We also went to the Coca Cola plant!" They were shocked at the memory coming back to them after all these years.
–RBP

The whole second grade was very excited. Our teacher, Miss Kondely, who very rarely smiled, was in a merry mood when she told us she had a surprise for us. All the children in the second grade were going on a trip to the Coca Cola plant in Manhattan. Buses had been supplied for us, and what's more, we were going to be served lunch: sandwiches and Coca Cola.

She told us that the night before we go we were all to take baths, have our hair neat and clean, wear newly pressed midi shirts, and have our red ties nicely tied under our collars.

"We have to make a good impression," she said, "and show the people at the Coca Cola plant that even though you are from immigrant parents, you can look as nice as real American children."

The day finally arrived, and we all gathered in the gym, spic and span, waiting for the buses. My mother had insisted that I take my lunch in a bag with me, as she was always worried that I would, God forbid, eat non-kosher food. I could not dissuade her, so I took the brown paper bag with my sandwich in it. But when I got to school I didn't see anyone else with their lunch, so I threw mine away.

Miss Kondely addressed the entire second grade in the gym over the loudspeaker. She said we must all be as quiet as mice. No one was allowed to speak to his or her neighbor. No one was permitted to speak on the bus, and of course when we got to the plant, anyone seen talking would be pulled out of line and not be able to go on the tour.

We were all duly warned and, being afraid of Miss Kondely's eagle eye, we were like frightened little mice, standing mutely waiting for the bus. This was exceptionally hard for me, as I didn't quite understand all the English spoken and would have asked my partner, Selma, whose mother called her Shayndl, to translate for me. So I stood there with the others, not completely understanding what was going on. The buses arrived, and we took our assigned seats without making a sound.

The bus ride was very interesting for me, as I was lucky enough to get a seat by the window, where I could see other streets and houses. I even saw some empty lots and trees. Where I lived we didn't have any. I wanted the bus to keep riding, but it stopped, and we all got off.

We entered a large waiting room of the Coca Cola plant. A tall man in a white coat came out and welcomed us in a pleasant voice. He said we all looked like very nice children and that he would take us on a tour of the plant and show us how Coca Cola is made and bottled. He told us that the recipe for Coca Cola was a great secret held by the family that owned Coca Cola. He also told us that Coca Cola was healthy for us and that all Americans drank it. It was the largest-selling drink in America.

We all went through the plant and saw the very large vats where they mixed the Coca Cola, and then we went into another room where they poured the liquid from funnels into the Coca Cola bottles. Then the bottles were covered with a metal cap by another machine. They moved by themselves on a narrow metal belt. By the time we got through seeing everything, we were tired and hungry.

The nice man said it was now time for us to have our lunch, and we went into a large lunchroom with many tables and benches. Then we got a little box that had a wrapped-up sandwich and an apple in it. We were all given a bottle of Coca Cola. I thought the bottle was very nice, and I couldn't wait to taste the soda. But first I unwrapped my sandwich and saw the whitest bread I had ever seen. It was really white, not like our rolls or challah. When I bit into it, it tasted like raw dough, and it stuck to the roof of my mouth. Then I tasted something very strange, like pasty smoked meat with some kind of cheese on it. I hated it and spit it out. I asked Shayndl very quietly what it was. She said she thought it was ham and cheese on

Tastee Bread. She was American-born, so she knew a lot of things. I couldn't eat my sandwich, not only because I hated it, but it wasn't even kosher.

When I tried the Coca Cola, it tasted like paint. I wanted to spill it out and keep the pretty bottle, but the teacher said we couldn't take the bottle with us, because it was glass, and it might break. Oh, how I wished I had taken my mother's sandwich! I came home hungry and tired, and I never told my mother about our Coca Cola lunch.

Jerusalem, My Mother's Dream

My youngest son, the one who spilled the earth on my mother's grave, still has the jar in a china closet. He considers it one of his treasures. –*RBP*

It all started with a song. I was sitting at the table one day humming a song to myself, not really aware of what I was humming, when my father, who was sitting opposite me, suddenly remarked, "How do you know that song?

"What song?" I answered absentmindedly. And then I began to put the words to the melody.

Kum Yisrolkl a heym, a heym
Tsu dayn sheynem libn land,
Nu kum zhe snel un kler keyn sakh,
Zay a folk mit felker glaykh,
Yisrolik, tate, sheneler kum a heym.

Come Yisrolikl, come home, come home,
To your beloved lovely land.
Quickly come, don't hesitate,
Have as others your own state,
Yisrolik, Father, quickly come, come home.

"Oh," I said, "Mama always sings that song. Haven't you heard her?"

My father looked a little sheepish. "I guess she doesn't sing it when I'm around," he said sadly. "Yes, yes," he continued with a sign. "Yes, I heard her sing it many times, long ago. I didn't realize she still sings it."

Sholem bayes, household peace, was not one of the strong points of our family. My mother and father were constantly at war with one another. They were, as we would say, a mismatched couple, yet in many ways our home was filled with warmth and affection. Individually, both my parents were admirable people. But put them together, it was like fire and water. As we grew older, we children—

there were three of us—would wonder how those two ever got together.

My mother was a Zionist, religious, ethical, intellectual. She was of a stoic nature, and her sense of humor had a long way to go to be anything more than a guarded smile. Though she seemed to have an iron will and was as stubborn as they come, she was afraid of change. She could not initiate anything. Still, she fought my father tooth and nail over any move he proposed. However, my mother always carried herself as though she came from aristocracy, and she was a beautiful woman.

My father, on the other hand, was a free thinker, who loved to eat, sing, dance and have a good time. He loved parties; he loved people; he dared anything, and though he found it difficult to read or write, he would tell us he was really smart, only he didn't have a head for learning. He would now be diagnosed as dyslexic, but that was then, and his feelings of inferiority, no matter the bravado he used to cover them, cut deeply into his soul.

My father greatly admired my mother for her reading ability, and his greatest pleasure was to have her read aloud to him. He was deeply interested in world affairs and had great respect for learning. I can still recall his admiration of her as she translated or interpreted the Hebrew words and Biblical comments so often used by the Yiddish writers in newspaper articles and books. And although my parents were constantly in a state of war, both wanting their own lifestyle, it was apparent to us that my father deeply loved my mother.

"You know," says my father, his face breaking into a bemused grin, "from the very beginning, I had trouble with your mother. I couldn't make up my mind. Should I or should I not marry her. She was so beautiful with her long blonde *tzop* (braid) hanging down her back. I couldn't keep my eyes off her; and she was smart, too. She studied Hebrew and Russian, and she was always reading. But we were so different. We had such different ideas. She was a *farbrente Zionistke*, a flaming Zionist. Always she wanted to go to *Palestina Yerushalayim*. That's where she wanted to go, Jerusalem. At least she wasn't a *chalutzke*, a pioneer, God forbid. She was too religious.

"There was a training farm for *chalutzim*, pioneers, just between

Wysockie and Minsk, where young people who wanted to go to help build *Erets Yisroel* would go to learn to become workers and farmers. You know, not too many Jews knew how to farm. The Russian government didn't allow them to own land. And how many Jews knew how to build houses or do the real heavy work? Too many of them were scholars, or if not that, they were poor tailors or shoemakers or, you should excuse the expression, businessmen.

"Your mother was not afraid of hard work; I knew that for sure. But she didn't like their ideas. They were too free for her; they wanted to share everything. The land, the work, the children, the husbands. Actually they were learning how to live together, how to grow things, build things. And when they weren't working, they were always singing and dancing. She just was too conservative, too religious.

"Your mother was in love with Jerusalem, with the idea of Jerusalem. To her, Jerusalem was the center of the world. 'The history, the nearness to God, the dreams, the *neshome fum dem Yiddishen folk,* the soul of the Jewish people,' she used to say.

"Men used to come to the shtetl to collect money for the *yeshives* there, for the schools of Jewish learning. Then there were other men who came asking for money for passage, because they wanted to go there to die. They wanted to go there so that when the *Moishiakh*, the Messiah, came, they wouldn't have to travel far to rise up again. Your mother gave them her hard-earned money, more than she could afford.

"When we were together, she would tell me from all the wonders from Jerusalem. How beautiful the hills looked with their special light, how the air was different there like no other place. How from all the ten most beautiful things in the whole world, Jerusalem got nine of them. You would think she saw it personally. She assured me that miracles took place in that city every day.

"I told her I wasn't interested in miracles in Jerusalem; I wanted to make my own miracles in America. I told her I would like Jews to be free like all other people. To be safe, to have the right to be Jews anywhere in the world. Palestine good, Jerusalem good, but give me America.

"She said she didn't like this; she said she wouldn't marry me and go to America. She wouldn't leave her parents for America. For Jerusalem, okay, but not for America. Well, I didn't know what to do. I was crazy about her, but I wasn't crazy. Maybe if she wanted to be a *chalutz*, I would think about it, but to go to study in Jerusalem was not for me.

"My friends all told me I was crazy; I shouldn't even think of marrying her. But my heart pulled me to her. I didn't know what to do, so I went to our Rebbe, who was a very smart man. Not *farnatished* (fanatic), a *weltlecher mensch*, a worldly man.

"The Rebbe knew who Dvoire Zietz was, and he said to me, 'Avrom Mayer, you will have a very hard time living with your Dvoire. I know she is a very nice, smart and lovely girl. But the two of you don't match. Think well before you do anything. But let me tell you, Avrom Mayer, if you do marry her, you will have exceptional children.'

"Nu," says my father with a smile and a hug, "the Rebbe was right. I *takke* had a hard life with your mother, but my children are *takke* exceptional." Who was I to disagree?

"Well," continued my father, "even at our wedding there was trouble. Why, you may ask? Because of your mother's Zionism. You see, her friends wanted the klezmer to play their Zionist songs, and to tell you the truth, they weren't very lively. Of course, my friends wanted them to play their songs, popular, lively, inspiring ones. So each one yelled at the musicians, and the one who yelled the loudest got the songs.

"Of course, the other side didn't like that, and with the help of a few glasses of wine and a drink or two of Slivowitz to heat matters up, some of the young hotheads started a fistfight. The police were called, and I had to spend the rest of the night at the police station straightening things out."

My father had a good laugh recalling that episode. We were so engrossed in our conversation that we had not noticed my mother standing patiently listening to my father's *bubbe meises*, or grandmother tales, as she called my father's rather fanciful stories.

"My Zionism had nothing to do with it," she said defiantly. "His friends were just a bunch of rowdies." And so it went.

In the late fifties, my parents went to Israel. They stayed with my Aunt Mirel, my father's sister, who, with her husband and three children, left the shtetl just a few short years before the great disaster overtook our whole family, our whole town. They settled in Jerusalem, the new section. One could not go into the old city, which was held by the Jordanians. My mother was broken-hearted. All these years she had longed to walk on those ancient streets. In her soul, the Jerusalem of myth and *midrash*, of yearning and redemption, of history and story still glowed. However, she was glad to finally be in Eres Yisroel, and she vowed that if the day ever came when all of Jerusalem was again one, she would return and see with her own eyes the places of her girlhood dreams.

After the 1967 war, my parents did return. They went to Jerusalem to attend the wedding of my cousin Jaffe, a Sabra born in Jerusalem to my Aunt Mirel. Jerusalem was by then reunited, new and old, one golden city, and my mother lived her dream.

On returning home, my mother brought many mementos of the city for all of us. As we looked at the many things in her suitcase, we noticed a small jar filled with what looked to us like plain ordinary earth.

"What is this?" we asked her.

"Soil from Jerusalem," she answered quietly. "Your father did not want to live in Israel. America is his land. What could I do, leave him and all of you and live by myself? So I brought some soil from Mirel's garden back with me to at least have a bit of Jerusalem here in our house."

My father was visibly moved by my mother's quiet answer, but always the jester, he jokingly added, "Well, children, when your mother passes into the other world, in another one hundred and twenty years, of course, don't forget to empty this jar of dirt on her grave. That way she will have the two Jerusalems together: the one in heaven and the one from the earth."

And that's just what we did. My youngest son remembered this incident, and at my mother's first *yartzeit*, when her headstone was erected, he took the jar which he had in his possession and sprinkled it on her grave.

"Here, Bubbe," he said. "Rest easy. Jerusalem is with you, now and forever."

The Coat

People often react strongly to a story even though it is different from their own experience. On hearing this story, my friend Miriam started to cry. She said, "What a sad story that is! My father died before I was born, and my mother was in the same economic circumstance. And yet I never had to face that kind of situation. I was always dressed like a little princess." –*RBP*

My father, thinking that I was not too bright because I could neither spell nor add a column right, decided I should learn a trade, and this I did.

Instead of going to James Monroe, the local high school in the Bronx where all my friends and classmates went, I attended Washington Irving High School in Manhattan, where I took courses in sewing and fashion design. Instead of walking to school with everyone I knew, it took me over an hour and a half walking and riding the subway, during rush hour, to get to school, where I knew no one and no one knew me.

I was not thrilled to be there. First of all, it was an all-girls school, and I craved the fun and excitement of having boys around. Secondly, I actually disliked sewing, which I was good at, while fashion illustration, which was more interesting, found me to be a rather mediocre student.

The only subjects I enjoyed and excelled at were my economics classes and English literature. At sixteen, I was already politicized. I joined the Foreign Affairs Club at school, where I participated in discussions of the state of the world and found myself to be one of two students to tout Socialism and Karl Marx—and I didn't even like the other girl. I resented learning about the whims of fashion and what the latest debutantes were wearing to their parties and balls when everyone I knew was suffering from the hardships of the Great Depression. We were lucky to be able to buy one new garment a year. It was not hard to become a radical during those days.

In 1938, the fascist dictator Franco, with the help of Hitler's Germany, was bombing the cities of the Spanish Republic, and the world looked the other way. In 1938, Japan invaded Manchuria, and the United States continued sending Japan our scrap iron, which was being converted into weapons. In 1938, Hitler was targeting the Jews of Germany with all kinds of violence and discrimination, spreading anti-Semitism over all of Europe, and the world looked the other way. In 1938, my mother trembled for the safety of our family in Poland, where anti- Jewish restrictions were being placed on the whole Jewish population.

In 1938, my work-weary mother and my frustrated father, who were at each other night and day, had no time or inclination to see my unhappiness. I was out of place at school, where there were no Jewish girls in my classes. I felt alien in my thinking, in my emotional response to what I was learning. My inability to spell and do math kept me imprisoned and made me feel stupid, immigrant and lost.

I hated the way I looked, I had a recurring case of acne, and I hated the fact that my wardrobe did not compare to what the others were wearing. I hated the sandwiches my mother made me take to school, which were always wet from the tomatoes she insisted on putting in. I longed for a peanut butter and jelly sandwich on white bread, which my mother looked on in disgust and refused to buy. She was always afraid that things were not kosher, and "who in their right mind would eat that terrible white stuff they call bread?" But I wanted to be American.

But more than anything, I hated that my brother, eight years old, and my sister, six, looked like two scared little rabbits when my parents started screaming at one another. And so one day, after a more than usually fierce argument, my father, out of control, took off his leather belt and threatened my mother with it, and I decided life wasn't worth living. So I went into the bathroom and swallowed a bottle of iodine.

In what seemed like only a few seconds, my whole body was on fire. I started screaming so loudly that my parents, still arguing, heard me and ran into the bathroom. On seeing what I had done, my father grabbed me and almost carried me down the stairs of our apartment into his newly purchased used Ford and drove me to the Lincoln Hospital emergency room. The doctors immediately started pouring some white chalky substance down my throat, and I, enveloped in pain and horror, blanked out.

When the burning subsided a little, I saw the kind and concerned face of a doctor, who kept reassuring me that I would be okay. "When you're feeling better, we will have a good talk," he said. "Don't worry; you are not alone. Your parents will help you. There is nothing so terrible that you should want to take your life."

I didn't know what he was talking about. Then it dawned on me that he thought I was pregnant. Why else would a girl of sixteen want to end it all? When I told the doctor and my parents about my precious virginity, which I had fought for night after night by debating with my boyfriend just how far one can go, they were astonished.

"Then why, why, did you do this to yourself?" they kept asking me. How could I explain all the complexities of my unhappy life when I hardly knew them myself? All I knew was that my parent's behavior was unbearable for me, and I said so.

My parents listened in disbelief. "For that you wanted to kill yourself?" they asked me, like they couldn't believe a minor thing like that could cause such a reaction. So I listed some other minor complaints, one of which was, of all things, my old coat, of which I was ashamed.

"I want a new one," I said.

"You didn't have to do this to yourself in order for us to buy you a new coat," said my father. "And as far as me and your mama always fighting, *nu*, we'll try to do better. So what kind of coat would you like? You know we don't have so much money." I knew exactly what they had, one hundred and fifty dollars, saved through skimping and doing without, but I didn't care. For once I was going to have something I really wanted.

I had saved up fifteen dollars by babysitting for a whole year, and my mother took out forty precious dollars from the bank, and off we went one day in November to buy me the coat of my dreams. I had it all arranged in my head. We would go to Lord & Taylor and buy the kind of coat I had sketched in my class at school, a princess-style coat with simple lines, brown, the color then in vogue, and of good material.

When my mother heard my plan of going to Lord & Taylor, the blood drained from her face. What *chutzpah*, what gall I had, she said, to even think of such a thing! Who did I think I was, Rockefeller's grandchild? We don't belong in such a fancy place. We could never afford their prices.

"But Ma," I said, "I saw an advertisement in the paper of the kind of coat I want, and the price was exactly what we have, fifty-five dollars."

For once, my mother overcame her own reluctance and what must have been unease, and we went to Lord & Taylor on Fifth Avenue.

We were both self-conscious walking into the store. It took a great deal of bravado on my part to make my mother feel a little more confident, as I felt exactly as she did. We went up to the coat department, and I asked to see the coat I saw in the papers. The sales person said that that coat was no longer available. She had just sold the last one the day before. However, she had a very similar one. Would I like to see it? I said I would. My mother sat on a chair, saying nothing.

Then the saleslady brought out what could only be described as the most beautiful coat I had ever seen. It was brown, princess-style, lovely fabric, and it had a little Peter Pan mink collar. I put it on and looked at myself in the mirror. I couldn't believe the image I saw there. A slender dainty young girl looked back at me. A real American girl.

"Mama, oh Mama, I want this coat!" I said. The saleswoman beamed.

My mother then said her first words. " How much is this coat?"

"It's only sixty dollars," the woman told her. "It too is on sale." My mother said nothing. She only looked at me, and I knew all was lost. Tears came into my eyes. The saleswoman saw what was happening and excused herself. So we could think it over, she said.

My mother looked at me with unusual kindness. "I know you love this coat. It looks very nice on you. But it is five dollars more than we have. If you ask me, it is not worth the money. Look at that tiny little fur collar! And the coat itself is so plain. But I'll tell you what. If you come with me to Fisher Brothers on the Lower East Side, where everyone goes for good buys, and you see what kind of coats they have, and if you still can't do without this coat, we'll come back here. Maybe they will hold the coat for you, and we'll find the other five dollars somewhere."

How could I refuse my mother's request, when it seemed so logical? But something in my heart told me I had lost my longed-for dream.

We went to Fisher Brothers, where my mother gloried in coats with lavishly trimmed fur collars, cuffs, and front panels. She made me try on a black one with black fur and stood in ecstasy looking at me.

All the ladies shopping at Fisher Brothers joined her in her joy at my appearance. "Look at her, a real model, you should put her in your window, Mr. Fisher, what a looker!" My mother was in seventh heaven as she pointed to the price tag hanging on the sleeve of the coat. It was ten dollars less than our fifty-five.

We bought the coat. It turned out to be dyed skunk, which had not been cured enough. It smelled to high heaven whenever it rained.

I hated that coat with all the anger and frustration of my young life. I hardly ever wore it. And to this day, I long for that princess-style brown coat with the little mink collar. Now that it could be mine, I'm much too fat for its simplicity.

Less Work for Mother

Several years ago, my sister and I went to the Museum of the City of New York. We wandered into a room and stood mesmerized, because there in the room was the Horn & Hardart automat. There was no one else there. And so my sister and I both simultaneously started to sing the jingle "Less Work for Mother." I said to my sister, "I have to tell my story." –*RBP*

Mother's Day was coming, and even though my mother pooh-poohed these made-up American holidays, I knew she would feel left out if I did not give her some kind of recognition on that day. Try as I could to save something out of the meager money given to me for subway fare to get to school and an occasional sandwich, all I was able to put aside for a Mother's Day gift was fifty cents.

Though I was resentful of my mother's constant demands on me to help around the house and be responsible for my brother and sister, I knew in my heart of hearts that she herself was overworked and under-appreciated for all she attempted to accomplish.

I really wanted to give her a Mother's Day present to tell her I wasn't as angry with her as I always sounded. I wanted to give her something that said I knew how hard she worked, and that I did appreciate her, even though she always yelled at me for not doing enough. But what could I buy her for fifty cents that had a meaning for both of us? One could actually buy something of worth for fifty cents in the 1930s, a scarf, a string of beads, but things like that were superfluous in my mother's life at that time.

Then I heard a jingle on the radio:

Less work for mother / Let's lend her a hand
Less work for mother / And she'll understand
She's your greatest treasure / Just make her life a pleasure
Less work for mother dear.

It was the advertisement of the Horn & Hardart company promoting the first venture into retail selling of their deliciously prepared food. The Horn & Hardart automats, as they were called, were a string of restaurants one could find in many of the busy sections of Manhattan. They were a favorite place to go to get a good cup of coffee out of a spigot in the wall, like a water fountain, for a nickel. The walls of the restaurant were surrounded with glass-enclosed little boxes that held a variety of delicious foods purchased by various amounts of nickels one had to insert into the accompanying slots alongside the glass windows, then the window opened up, and you took out your food.

In back of the wall of boxes were workers who kept feverishly refilling the foods purchased. One never saw them. To young children, it felt like magic. I loved their baked beans, the cost of which was two nickels. These beans were baked in a brown little crock pot and had a sugary brownish crust. I once tasted their apple pie, and I was transported to heaven. I couldn't afford to buy a slice, four nickels was much too expensive for my budget. Horn and Hardart was a great place to eat, no matter how much or how little you could afford, and one could sit there all day long, if that's what you wanted to do. The food was wholesome, fresh and delicious, and what fun to help yourself to such wonderful tasty treats, if you really had some money. That was the kind of food their retail stores were supposed to be selling. What a great idea, I thought. My mother, who never wanted to go to a restaurant, would have something delicious brought to her. I was going to buy her a Horn & Hardart's apple pie for Mother's Day.

After searching around for one of their stores, I found one not too far from my high school in Manhattan. On the way home, I entered the store and surveyed what was being offered for sale. There were foods there I did not recognize. The store felt intimidating, super-clean, reserved, and Gentile. I was almost afraid to speak to the woman behind the counter.

"Do you have apple pie for sale?" I asked her in a trembling voice.

"We certainly do," she answered, with a friendly smile. She brought out a lovely-looking pie, just the kind I wanted.

"How much is it?" I asked.

"Only one dollar; it's a special for Mother's Day."

My heart sank. "I only have fifty cents," I said, and turned to leave.

"Just a moment, honey. We have an individual one for one person, and it's only fifty cents." I bought the individual one just for my mother, and I couldn't wait to see her taste that wonderful pastry.

The day was Mother's Day, and just before supper I handed her the prettily wrapped package. My mother smiled and unwrapped the pie. I watched as a look of what one could call horror spread across her face.

"What is this?" she asked holding out the pie.

"It's a Horn & Hardart apple pie. It's very delicious, and I bought it just for you."

"How much did you pay for it?" asked my mother in her prosecutorial voice.

"Fifty cents."

"Fifty cents!" cried my mother. "For fifty cents I could have made three pies! And you bought it at Horn & Hardart's, a *goyishe*, Gentile store, so it isn't even kosher!"

"What's not kosher about a pie?" I asked.

"The crust, the crust is absolutely made with pig fat! Here, take it away!" says my mother, as if holding it another moment would kill her.

I took the pie back with a wound in my heart that took many years to heal. "All right," I shouted, "if you won't eat it, I will!" But before I could put my mouth on the crust, my mother smacked it out of my hands.

"I said it was not kosher!" My mother spoke through clenched teeth, as the pie fell on the floor. I picked up the squashed pie, and with a loud cry, I started to run out of the house. As I turned to go out of the door, I saw my mother, with tears running down her cheeks, raising her hand up to her face.

Many years later, when I recalled that episode to my mother, I saw tears again in my mother's eyes.

"I know why I cried, Mama," I said. "But why did you cry?"

"I cried," said my mother, "because I realized that I was so worn out, so tired, so unhappy, that I forgot to be a human being."

I Loved My Mother on Saturdays

When I told some of my stories to a fellow storyteller, she said, "Roslyn, your mother always appears as the villain in your stories. Didn't you like your mother at all?" And I said, "Yes, on Saturdays, I loved my mother." And she said, "That's a great story; you're going to have to write it." So here it is. –RBP

I loved Saturday, not because it was Shabbes, a day that brought back wonderful memories of my childhood in the shtetl; not because there was no school; not because you dressed up in your best clothes; not because you went to the movies. I loved Saturday because on that day, I loved my mother.

All through the week, my mother was a tight-tensioned wire coil, ready to spring at any moment. She hardly ever smiled; her sense of humor was completely nil. She could not handle anything that was the least bit negative in the life of her children. My mother worked four days a week with my father in his kosher butcher shop. She hated every minute of it. She was the exact opposite of my father, who did not mind cheating a little here and there, so the family could stay alive during the Great Depression. Whereas my mother would not go off the straight and narrow path even if we had to starve. They continually fought the battle of expediency versus ethics.

My mother would have like to stay home and feed her children healthy kosher food, instead of throwing things together at the last moment. My mother would have loved to go to night school to learn to read and write English as well as she read and wrote Hebrew, Yiddish and Russian. My mother would have liked to spend her evenings reading books of philosophical value, instead of washing clothes, mending socks, ironing. My mother was good at whatever task she undertook: sewing, cooking, baking. She made curtains for all our windows. She made summer covers for our couch and armchairs. Anything and everything that needed doing attained perfection in her hands. Under the load of all her labors, she was continually stressed out and frustrated, day and night.

On Friday, my mother was a complete tyrant and hysteric. It was the only day she did not go into the store. Everything had to be done on that one day to prepare for the Shabbes, which started at sundown on Friday night. Being dogmatic and attached to the routine of shtetl life, she would not deviate one iota from the rituals, customs and requirements mandated for celebrating that holy day.

Friday was my nightmare day. On my return from school, I had to change all the bed linens, polish the furniture, whisk-broom the couch and arm chairs, and polish the floors. Then we all had to take our baths, put on clean clothes, and wait for the beginning of the Shabbes meal.

My mother was a virtual tornado in the kitchen. She baked challah, an egg bread one needed for the blessing of the grain. She baked various kinds of cake. The chicken and the accompanying chicken soup was put up to boil; the noodles waited for their turn. My mother made her own gefilte fish, a kind of fish cake eaten on holidays, or chopped liver. She made her own applesauce or compote. She made sure we had the sweet red wine needed for the blessing. After cooking, she put a clean white cloth on the table, washed the kitchen floor, took her own bath, and was ready to light the Shabbes candles just as the sun went down. Her face was always flushed from heat generated by the stove, her own frenzy to accomplish this Herculean task before sundown, and the warm bath needed to be clean for the beginning of Shabbes.

My father on the other hand came home tired from his chores, and he was not interested in following my mother's routine. He balked at taking his bath just at that time, or changing his clothes, or going to the synagogue, or even saying all the prayers mandated for Shabbes. And so there was a bitter fight almost every Friday night, which was just the opposite of the spirit of the holiday.

But oh, what a difference Saturday made! On that day, my mother was the Shabbes Queen. The *Shekhinah*, the gentle spirit of God, ruled our house. I don't ever remember my parents at war with one another on Shabbes. My mother's face took on a quiet look of peace. The tensions of the work-weary week faded from her eyes; they now had a gentle sparkle. She even smiled when my father said something to amuse us.

The house itself became a welcoming haven, offering us the wonderful aroma of last night's feast. A feeling of cleanliness that emanated from the furniture polish and floor wax pervaded every room. And when my mother rose from her bed, combed her hair and put on her holiday clothes, her aristocratic bearing somehow suited the occasion.

And all day long until sunset, my mother went about her usual activities allowed on the Shabbes with a serenity that gave us all a measure of contentment. The highlight of the day was when my mother came home from the synagogue, and we had our dinner of cold chicken. You are not allowed to cook or do any manual labor on Saturday, so my mother would open the Jewish newspaper and read to my father some of the articles they both found interesting. In a household where there is always turmoil and contention between the parents, it is a gift to the children to see their parents in harmony, even if it is only for the one day set aside by tradition for rest and contemplation.

I loved my mother on Saturdays, and I loved Saturdays because they showed me my mother the way I always wanted her to be.

Graf Ptotski's Eynikl

When I tell this story in senior centers, there are always some people who know the expression "Graf *Ptotski's* eynikl," *and they get such a kick out of hearing it.*
–RBP

Have you ever heard of Graf Ptotski? No? Well, let me tell you about him. Graf, or Count, Valentin Ptotski was a very rich and famous Polish nobleman who lived in what is now known as Belarus, White Russia. He was renowned among the Jews because he was said to have been very friendly to them. There were many legends about him throughout the Jewish Pale. One legend told of his conversion to Judaism; another that he was burned at the stake by the Church for heresy. Stories were written about him telling of his kind deeds and noble actions.

My acquaintance with the name Graf Ptotski, however, was on a much more familiar basis. You see, every time I wanted something that was out of reach, something my mother thought quite impossible to accomplish, she would say to me, "Who do you think you are, Graf Ptotski's *eynikl*? Graf Ptotski's grandchild?" And, in all the shtetlach, the little towns of that region, when someone had a dream, a plan of getting somewhere in the world, somewhere beyond shtetl expectations, the scoffers, skeptics, would point their skinny fingers and say, "Who does he think he is, Graf Ptotski?"

But Graf Ptotski was more than just a legend or folk expression to the people of my town; to us he was real and tangible. There was a beautiful vacant and rundown estate with an adjacent forest right outside of town. The forest was open to the inhabitants on Saturdays and Sundays. To tell the truth, no one was sure to whom it really belonged, so why not Graf Ptotski? It was called "Graf Ptotski's forest."

This magnificent forest was one of the blessings of the Shabbes to our little town. Every Friday afternoon, I would accompany my Aunt Shoske to Berel the baker, where we would put into his oven the *cholent* my grandmother made. This was a stew which cooked for twenty-four hours. The baking ovens were banked on Friday before sundown, as there was no baking or cooking done on Shabbes. The oven, however, remained red-hot until sundown the next day. For a small fee of a few *groshn*, the baker would allow the townspeople to put their cholent into the oven until Saturday afternoon, where it was brought forth in all its glory, to be eaten after davening, after praying at the synagogue.

The family would then sit down to eat the Shabbes meal, sing *zmires*, psalms, after eating. Then my grandmother and grandfather would take a nap. My aunts, uncle, and their friends, along with most of the young people of the town, would go for a walk, a *shpatsir*, on the town's main street, *oyfn forshtot*, which brought them directly to the glorious forest of Graf Ptotski.

And what a forest it was—full of white birch trees! When the sun shone on their delicate little leaves and embraced their white etched trunks, the forest glowed with a silvery golden light. It became an enchanted fairy world. For me, the forest was the place where the angels lived when they weren't up in heaven. No one raised their voices there, but spoke in quiet tones about lofty subjects, or so it seemed to me.

I would go there with my aunts and uncle to sit on the soft velvety green grass and fall asleep to their hushed melodic conversations. In later years when things became difficult for me, I would travel back in my mind to that faraway forest of my childhood and still find comfort and solace there.

Coming of age in New York and for years after, I hadn't thought about Graf Ptotski. After all he wasn't part of my scheme of things until one of my sons decided that he had to go this exclusive private school in Lenox, Massachusetts.

"Who do you think you are?" I said to him, "Graf Ptotski's grandchild?"

"Who?" says my son.

"Never mind," I say, "go on." Well, it seemed that someone told him he was a great dramatic talent and he could easily get a scholarship for free tuition.

And you know what? He did. So away he went to Windsor

Mountain School in the lovely Berkshire Hills, where actors and actresses send their children, where the children of ambassadors and bankers go, and where he met Steven Schul.

Steven Schul was the child of Robert and Ethel Schul, who owned a large fleet of yellow taxi cabs called Schul's Angels. You may have seen them in Manhattan. Steven's mother Ethel was a personal friend of Andy Warhol, who had painted a series of pictures of her. Both Mr. and Mrs. Schul were avid collectors of Pop Art and knew all the right people.

Their son Steven and my son Bobby became bosom buddies. On one of the school holidays, Bobby was invited to their home for the weekend, where he met Mr. Schul. In one of their conversations together, Mr. Schul told Bobby that his father had been born in Grodno Gubernia, and that their family comes from aristocracy.

When Bobby related this to me, I burst out laughing. I had never heard of Jewish aristocracy from Grodno Gubernia. "You'll see for yourself," says my son, "when you meet Steven's father at the play I'm directing."

Sure enough, on the following Sunday, I am introduced to Robert Schul, a tall, good-looking man of about fifty. After the usual pleasantries, Mr. Schul addresses me directly and to the point. "Mrs. Perry, your son tells me you were born in Grodno Gubernia."

"Yes," I said, "in a shtetl called Witoskie Litewsk, which is in the province of Grodno."

Mr. Schul smiles condescendingly. "My father was also born there."

"Do you know the town?" I ask him. "We may even be related."

Mr. Schul isn't amused. "I don't know the town," he says with great dignity, "but I know we come from aristocracy."

"Oh!" I say, definitely put in my place.

"My father," Mr. Schul says, squaring his shoulders, "was Graf Ptotski's *eynikl*."

"Graf Ptotski's what!" I say stunned.

Mr. Schul now looks quizzically at me and repeats his pedigree. "Is anything wrong?" he asks.

"No, no," I lie, "it's just that I know that name very well."

"You know Graf Ptotski?" he asks in amazement.

"No, not personally, but I used to walk in his forest as a child."

"You don't say!" beams Mr. Schul with great pride. "You don't say."

And I didn't say. I didn't say that his father was as much Graf Ptotski's *eynikl* as my father was John D. Rockefeller. I didn't say, because I myself was shocked at what arrogance and ignorance can create. And I didn't say that Graf Ptotski, the one the Jews loved, the one whose *eynikl* everyone would have loved to be, was born in the eighteenth century. Of course I didn't say; I didn't want to burst his bubble. You see, I needed a ride back to New York.

Food Is More Than Eating

This story was picked up by the famous Second Avenue Delicatessen in the book published on the recipes of the restaurant. It was one of the four stories the cookbook writers requested. *-RBP*

Food is more than eating, my grandfather used to say. Food is for remembering who you are, what you are, where you came from. And what is more important, with food, you follow God's commandments, and you celebrate His name.

My grandfather spoke the truth. All shtetl life revolved around religious observances and festivals in which food played a very important part. My mother, who had a difficult time acclimating herself to her new life in America, held onto the old country ways, especially in relation to the serving of food for the holidays. She followed the routine her mother and her mother's mother had followed.

Every holiday had its own special menu. We knew what holiday we were celebrating by the delectable smells emanating from the kitchen. She kept the old country alive for us by her meticulous adherence to what she called her duty. This consisted of her reciting with great pleasure why we eat the various foods on a particular holiday.

"You should always remember," says my mother, "that we eat the little cakes called *hamentashen* on Purim because it is a mitzvah, a good deed, to thank God that the Jews were saved by the beautiful Queen Esther and her wise uncle Mordekhai from the terrible wrath of that arch villain Haman.

"But why are they called *hamentashen*, and why are they shaped that way?" I asked.

"I don't know," says my mother. "They were always shaped that way."

On Simkhas Toyre, my mother piled the *kreplakh* high on our plates, adding her usual sermon.

"Remember that we eat *kreplakh* on Simkhas Toyre because we are happy that God gave us the Toyre."

"Why *kreplakh*, Mama?" I asked.

"Because," chants my father, "because *kreplakh* are good and Toyre is good."

"Remember," intones my mother on Hanukkah, "we eat *latkes* on this day to celebrate the great victory of the Jewish heroes, the Maccabees, over the mighty Roman legions."

"Why *latkes?"* I ask.

"I really don't know," says my mother, "and I don't think it's so important that you should always want to know *fun vanen di fis vaksn*—from where your legs start to grow. Why must you understand everything?"

My father, seeing my disappointment over this answer, compounds my indignation by telling me that since Hanukkah is the season for lighting Hanukkah candles and it deals with fire, we eat *latkes* so that the burning of the candles on the outside should correspond to the heartburn you get from eating them on the inside.

This answer convinced me that I had to find another source outside of the family to really find out why we eat *latkes* on Hanukkah. So after asking many relatives and friends of my parents who did not know, I finally found a *landsman*, a countryman, who explained it all to me.

His name was Yudl-Leybke. He was a favorite of all of us children as he was the only one of our parents' friends who deemed us important enough to talk to.

"So," says Yudl-Leybke, "you really want to know why we eat latkes on Hanukkah, do you? So sit yourself down, and I'll tell you a story.

"In the spring, all the little animals are born. The baby cows, the baby horses, goats, ducks, geeses. In America, they call the baby geeses *goslings,* but in Europe we called them *gendzelakh.* So all summer long, the *gendzelakh* swim around with their mama. They eat little fishes and all kinds of grasses, and they grow up to be beautiful geeses."

"Geese," I correct him.

"All right," he says, "geeses. What are you going to do with so many of them, because the winter is coming? So you take them to the *shaykhet*, the ritual slaughterer, and slaughter them. The nights are getting longer, and what is there to do at night in the shtetl? So all the women and the young girls sit around the stove and pluck the geeses to get the beautiful white *pukh* we call "down." They use the down to make *perenes*, feather beds and pillows, so that the girls getting married will have them as part of their trousseau, part of their dowry. Then the fat from the geeses is rendered and made into delicious goose *shmaltz. Shmaltz* you can keep for a long time in the cold weather. The geeses are roasted for Shabbes, and everyone is happy.

"By now it's already Hanukkah. Everyone likes to go out to visit each other on Hanukkah, to play cards, spin the *dreidl*, light Hanukkah candles, sing songs. So what are you going to serve them? Potatoes, we got plenty. So you grate the potatoes, grate in some onion, add salt, pepper, an egg, a little bit of flour or matzo meal, then fry the *latkes* in that wonderful goose fat.

"Oy, oy, oy!" he says, "I can still feel the taste of those *latkes* in my mouth today. Nobody knows who started serving *latkes* on Hanukkah, but if you ask me, whoever did it was a very smart person."

I must tell you, I was not at all pleased with his answer. I wanted something much more lofty. But as I got older, I realized that customs arise from very practical sources. People, however, need a little romance, a few miracles with their sustenance, and the myth, the legend, the story, comes into being.

So why do we eat *latkes* on Hanukkah? We eat them because we have always eaten them.

So tell me, would you have it any other way?

My Father and the Cow Udders

I told this story at an informal gathering on the first night of a visit to Havana for a storytelling festival and conference. The other storytellers, all from Spanish-speaking countries, were sharing bawdy stories. At least that's what my translator told me. So I asked her to translate this one into Spanish. I can tell you, I had a hard time explaining to her what an udder was! But hand gestures, the universal language, finally did the trick.

–RBP

My father was a fun-loving, daring, self-indulgent, hard-working man with a fierce temper. He once told me that he was very smart, but he didn't have a head for learning. Actually, my father was dyslexic, but who knew about dyslexia in those days? He could just about read the Jewish newspaper, and he had a very hard time reading his prayer book. He also found it difficult dealing with numbers, all of which added up to a rather poor opinion of himself. But my father was smart, even though he would never learn to read or write English. He was a wheeler-dealer, a hail-fellow-well-met, imaginative, and a great admirer of nature, so much so that he would proudly bring home flowers that he gathered from park plantings that said, "Do not pick." When he went fishing in the Hudson River, he told us of the many fish that practically begged to be caught. But he knew my mother would only fry two, and so that's the amount he brought home.

When he arrived here in America, New York to be exact, his name was Avrom Mayer Kolner. But on hearing of a very successful wholesale meat market whose proprietors were the Max Kollner brothers, he changed his name to Max Kollner, figuring that it didn't hurt to have the same well-respected name. And, he added with great satisfaction, since everyone called him Maychic, a Slavic derivative, which sounded like Max, and since he too dealt in meat, something good might come of it. The only thing that *did* happen was that sometimes he would receive a letter or two of their mail by mistake, which he personally returned to them. He actually got to know them and asked them for employment, but was politely refused due to his inability to read and write English.

My father was not too particular about propriety or truth, which, he said, was relative. Although he was truly a generous man, fun-loving, with a gift of gab, his standing with my mother was less than accepting. And so this incident I am going to relate should be taken with a grain of salt.

"It was Friday evening. Our Shabbes, Sabbath, begins the night before, and my mother was very committed to following all the ceremonies and rituals that are accorded to this holy night. We were impatiently waiting for my father to come home so we could start the Shabbes meal. He was already an hour late. My mother had said the blessing after lighting the Shabbes candles, and we were sitting around a set table waiting for him. In he comes with a smile on his face and tells us this story:

"Today is Friday, and as you know, I clean up the butcher shop and then go downtown to the slaughterhouse to buy meat for the week. Well, I finished giving them my order and was on the way out, when I saw this barrel standing right at the door of a very long hallway. As I walked by I looked inside the barrel. It had no cover on it, and something familiar caught my eye. It was cows' udders.

"I looked at the udders and my mouth started to water as I remembered how wonderful they tasted. Here in America I never saw them being sold. They must use them for animal food. In Europe we always ate them because they are kosher. So I decided that I wanted to buy one. Mama could cook it for me. You know they taste just like Italian food, meat that has the taste of cheese with it."

"How do you know the taste of Italian food?" my mother demanded to know in her usual voice of disgust at my father eating non-kosher food.

"All right, all right a'ready," says my father. "Don't you want to hear my story?" My mother nods silently.

"So I look around for someone to sell me the udder. There's no one around, so I take one anyway. Then I look around for something to wrap it in. There is nothing. I don't want to put the udder back, so I get this idea and stick it into my pants. It's soft, so I tighten my belt to hold it in place, and I head for the subway.

"So I'm sitting on the subway reading my paper, and I feel someone is staring at me. I look up, and I see two women sitting across the aisle looking at me with their mouths open and horror on their faces. They seem to be looking at my crotch. So I look at my crotch and—*es is mir gevoren shartz in de oygen*—I nearly blacked out. My zipper had moved down, and one of the teats was sticking out. I couldn't move my zipper up, and I certainly couldn't move it down, and the women were staring at me like you never saw. So I took out my pocket knife, and I cut it off.

"One woman started to scream, and the other one started to faint. So I ran over to them and said, 'Ladies, ladies, don't worry! I have three more where this comes from.' So you know what? A third lady also started screaming. Someone called a policeman, and I had a hard time trying to explain this to him. That's why I'm late."

Sitting at the table and listening to my father, we couldn't stop laughing. When we caught our breath, we all accused my father of making up this cock and bull story. Then my father with great dignity reaches into his pants and pulls out an udder with one teat missing.

To this day, we don't know if he made up the story and cut the teat off himself to make it authentic, because he refused to discuss it any further. Suffice it to say, the udder was sautéed and tasted great—just like Italian food, only a bit more Jewish.

A New World

From New York with Love

Finkie, the woman in the story, now lives in an assisted living facility. When I went to visit her, her children came in from New Orleans. Somehow the conversation turned to the story that I wrote about the shivah *for their father. The daughters-in-law hadn't heard the story. "Roslyn, tell us the story!" they said. I told them the story, and they looked at me like I'd made up something great. They turned to Finkie and asked, "Was that true?" She said, "I swear by my children it happened!"* -*RBP*

Death is a terribly searing and hurtful experience, even when the person who has gone is not necessarily a close member of the family or even a best friend, but is someone liked and appreciated.

Such a one was my daughter-in-law's Uncle Anch, from New Orleans. My daughter-in-law is from New Orleans. She was one of the pleasant surprises presented to our family by my youngest son when he announced that he had found a girl with whom he could share his life.

With a wicked twinkle he told us she was a Southern girl, good-looking, very intelligent, very talented and very independent. Then with a big grin, he added the additional information that she was also Jewish. He knew this would please my mother no end, and it didn't make the rest of us unhappy, either. It felt good knowing that she was one of us even though she came from New Orleans.

There was an additional bonus to this relationship, and that was her family. After all, how could I resist a *makhatensiste*, that's a Yiddish word for the bride's mother, who on first meeting me exclaimed with glee, "Y'all can see where Bobby gets his good looks!" It was love from the very beginning.

And not only were Leslie's parents a joy, but her Aunt Finkie and Uncle Anch, without whom her parents never moved, were two of the most charming people one had the good fortune of knowing.

Leah, Leslie's mother, and Finkie, her sister, were two lovely-looking women. Soft-spoken with a delightful Southern drawl. Sam, Leslie's father, was the more serious, studious, straight man to her Uncle Anch, who was the patriarch of the family and an outrageous jokester. It was a treat when they came to New York to visit.

Anch always brought a funny story or joke to tell me. As it turned out, I had always already heard it before. Being a fashion designer in the garment industry is a sure bet of knowing the latest jokes and stories making the rounds. You see, no vendor or salesman ever comes to sell you something without first saying, "Have you heard this one?"

This, however, did not discourage Anch, who when seeing by the expression in my eyes that I had already had the pleasure, would remark with Southern charm, "frankly, my dear, I don't give a damn; you'll just have to hear it again."

Once, during one such visit, our *makhatonin*, that's plural in Yiddish for the family of one's in-laws, greatly admired a jogging suit I was wearing. On discovering that it was one that I designed and that it was being manufactured by my firm, both women expressed their desire to buy one. Magnanimously rejecting their offer to buy, I proudly offered to have our factory send them each one. "If it isn't asking too much," said Finkie modestly, "is it possible for you to send one for my daughter-in-law, too?"

"Certainly," I answered with congenial generosity. It wasn't costing me anything.

So the very next day I called Vesti, the woman who was in charge of shipping in one of our plants in Johnson City, Tennessee, gave her the address, and told her to send the jogging suits. One small, one medium and one large.

"What color do you want in what size?" asked Vesti.

"Oh, I don't know," I answered, not wanting to be bothered. I was always rushed for time.

"Send them an assortment."

"Okay," says Vesti.

Several weeks later I get a call from Leah and Finkie. They are both on the line laughing hysterically, unable to make themselves understood because they can't stop laughing.

"What's so funny?" I want to know.

"The jogging suits," they manage to squeak out between howls, "we're drowning in jogging suits, all colors, all sizes. Do you intend for us to go into business? How will we get rid of them? Because if we give them to our friends, we will all be wearing the same thing. We don't know about you gals in New York, but down here we don't go in for uniforms."

Well, it seemed that when I told Vesti to send them an assortment, she sent them a dozen of each, as they were packed small, medium, and large, assorted for color to each size.

This incident was never forgotten by our New Orleans connections, and they were very careful not to ask me for any other item. Anch especially made that story part of his repertoire of tales.

Time takes its toll and Anch, who had not been well when we first met, became gravely ill. Full of suffering and pain, he mercifully passed away. It was a bitter thing for all who knew him. He was a very special man.

What can you say or do when you are so many miles away? How do you hold out your hand in friendship to comfort, to embrace, to cry, even to laugh with those whose world will never be the same?

"Sitting *shiva,*" the seven days of mourning practiced by Jews on the death of a member of the family, is a ritual endowed with great emotional healing. For seven days the family is not to engage in any of the everyday activities of normal life. They live through their loss. Friends and relatives prepare their meals. No work is allowed. Prayers are said twice a day by a minyan, a quorum, of ten men. The custom is for people to visit the mourners, talk about the departed, remember his uniqueness, recall anecdotes concerning him. And so there is often laughter along with the tears.

But how does one participate in this loving ritual when you are 2,000 miles away? It would have felt good if I, too, could be the bearer of food, not only for the body, but for the soul, as well.

And then the thought came to me. "Why not?" So during my lunch hour I hurriedly got myself over to the Lower East Side of Manhattan, to a world-famous Jewish delicatessen, Katz's, on Houston Street, and ordered two large salamis, one whole pastrami, three Jewish rye breads with seeds, sliced, eight potato knishes, two jars of kosher dill pickles from the pickle barrel and two large containers of mustard.

With three enormous shopping bags I hailed a cab and back to my office I went. I wrapped each item carefully in tissue paper, then in newspaper, put everything into one of the cartons we use for sending out samples, stuffed it with white cotton fabric to make sure everything was securely in place, and told the mail boy to send this box off Federal Express, overnight mail to New Orleans, pronto! Well, I must tell you the cost of that mailing was more than what I had paid for the food. But my firm could afford it, even if I couldn't. And so it went!

Several days later my phone rang. It was Finkie. I hardly recognized her voice. She sounded so tired, so full of pain.

"I had to call you," she said. "I haven't called another soul, but I had to talk to you. I must tell you what you did for me.

"I don't have to tell you how I have been feeling," she said mournfully. "It has been a total nightmare from beginning to end. After the funeral, I walked around in a complete daze. I guess I did the right things, said the right things, but I didn't know what was happening. I couldn't bear to really know what was going on.

"There were so many people coming and going, there was so much activity, that one day I didn't want to come down from my bedroom. I didn't want to face another person. Agnes, my housekeeper, was busy in the kitchen when your package arrived. She called up to me and asked me what to do with this large box that had just arrived from New York.

"Who is it from?" I asked, and she told me it was from The House of Ronnie, your firm. I knew it was yours. Bring it up here, I told her. Why in heaven's name, I thought, was Roslyn sending me more jogging suits? I really had no patience to look at anything, and it felt so inappropriate.

"'Put it in the closet,' I told Agnes. 'I'll look at it some other time.'

"The next morning as I was getting dressed, I thought I smelled something cooking. I called down to Agnes and asked her what she was making that had such a strong garlic smell. I wasn't in the mood for that kind of food. In fact, I wasn't in the mood for anything.

"Agnes answered that she wasn't cooking anything, not even water. 'Come up here,' I told her, 'there is definitely a smell of food up here.'

"Agnes came up and started to smell around. She agreed with me that there was a smell of garlic. She called my sister Leah to come up, and several other people joined her upstairs. Everyone started sniffing around to see where the smell was coming from. And then someone opened the closet, and the smell almost knocked us over.

"'It's coming from that large box in the closet,' said Leah. Agnes took out the box, opened the top, and I reached in it. And from under the white cotton cloth, I pulled out one of the largest salamis I had ever seen.

"There I stood in the middle of the room, holding up the salami, not knowing if I should laugh or cry. Then everyone started reaching into the box, pulling out another salami, pastrami, bread, pickle, all the food Anch loved so much, and before I knew what was happening, I was laughing. At first the laughter was laced with tears, but then, as everyone joined in, the laughter became real and honest. I was laughing at the ridiculousness of life. At its pain and joy, at the tragicomedy we are all involved in. And I awoke from my nightmare to face what I had to.

"'From New York with Love,'" your note said, "And now I say, thank you, my friend."

All in a Day's Work

Not long after I made this story part of my repertoire, I told it at a festival on Long Island. Imagine my surprise to see the salesman whose name I had mixed up sitting in the audience! After the storytelling hour was over, I took some of the other storytellers with me to introduce him to them. We both embraced each other with much laughter, and then, as I turned to introduce him, I couldn't remember his name.

"This man," I said with bravado, "is called the juice of life."

Then he added with great satisfaction, "My name is inside of what makes every guy's life worth living."

-RBP

On August 30, 1987, I officially retired as senior fashion designer from a leisure and sportswear firm situated in the garment district of New York City. I worked there for thirty-three years. They were, on the whole, exciting and satisfying years. And though new partners joined the organization as the company expanded, I primarily worked with the same people over that period of time.

In the garment industry, especially in a firm that puts such emphasis on fashion, this is, I must say with some sense of modesty, a record. My longevity on the job was not, however, due to my outstanding talent, to which I readily admit, but to the fact that I was a student of human behavior and I have a "big mouth," as my boss so often told me.

You must know that the New York garment industry is primarily a Jewish-run industry at the top. Once upon a time from the turn of the century to the second World War, most of the workers were also Jewish along with many Italians and a smattering of Poles. Today, however, only the bosses and salesmen are Jewish. The New York clothing industry is now a far cry from what it once was. Its manufacturing facilities have relocated to the far east, to the southern states, to California, and it is now being challenged by many other countries from around the world.

"So what's the story?" you may ask. Well, the story is how I managed to stay in this volatile industry for thirty-three years and what was asked of me. "It's all in a day's work," my boss used to say.

The man who first discovered me was Morris. He was a perfect example in many ways of the type of man who first established the small clothing factories of New York City. Exceptionally bright, with a gift of gab, he, like so many others like him, had no real formal education. He just about made it to the sixth grade before he had to start working to help support the family. He, however, wore his ignorance like a shield of honor, often boasting to us more educated folks, that he is where he is, because of that fact.

Actually he was worldly-wise, self-educated, with a natural dignity and an intellectual curiosity.

But wait a minute, I'm getting ahead of my story. How did we grow? Why did we expand?

Because of me, of course! Morris trained me not only to design petticoats that were irresistible to the low-income customer, but he also trained me to make the type of styles that the limited machinery of the plant was able to manufacture. The petticoats sold for one dollar retail. We were an instant success with my first try. To me that petticoat looked liked a monstrosity. It came in three colors, fuchsia, orange and kelly green covered with black lace. It sold like hot cakes. It was a winner!

After that triumph, all the important people in the shop knew I had an unusual talent and was indispensable to the firm. Morris then decided that I not only do the designing, but that I now also see suppliers in order to choose fabrics and laces. He also felt that I should acquaint myself with the buyers in order to help with the selling. He lectured me on the right approach to these people.

He had observed, he told me, that I was too logical, too reasonable. "You will never be effective at getting what you want, which at times will be the impossible, by being so understanding. Throw a fit sometimes, act temperamental; after all you're an artist, you're allowed." I must tell you I really tried, but the only person with whom I could act that way was Morris himself, so we gave that one up.

Morris taught me how to smoke, drink martinis and carry on small talk with the buyers. You have to look and act the part, he would say. "It's all in a day's work."

I don't remember if I told you before, but I'm dyslexic. That's how I found my way into the garment industry. In the first place, if I was able to spell or do math or know my left from my right or remember names, places, dates and other such important things, I could have become, God knows what! At my job I didn't have too much trouble with my inability to spell; no one wanted me to write anything anyway. The pattern maker helped me out with my math, especially fractions. But my not remembering names really got me into hot water.

Once I sampled some great material from a firm called Jaftex. The leisure coat made from that fabric got into the line, and we were preparing to start production. I was not allowed to submit the order for the cloth. First because I couldn't figure out how many yards we would need, and secondly because my boss could not trust me with getting the lowest price possible for the fabric. Don't forget, I was too reasonable. You see, when a salesman told me that the price was absolutely the lowest he could go, I believed him.

Well, anyway, Morris asks me who the salesman was that submitted the sample cloth to us. I can't remember his name, and the tag on the cloth is torn off and lost. Morris tries to keep calm, but he is having a hard time.

"Think, think," says my boss. "I have to deal with somebody!" Well I thought and I thought and then I remembered. His name is Seaman, yes, Mr. Seaman. Morris calls the cloth company and asks for Mr. Seaman. The receptionist informs him that there is no such person there. "There must be," says Morris, becoming agitated.

"There isn't," says the receptionist, now also agitated. Morris calms down. "Okay, okay," says Morris, "let's see if we can solve this. Can you kindly tell me the names of your salesmen? Maybe my designer will recall which one of them came to see her." She lists the names, and he repeats them to me. He goes through about four names that were definitely not right, and then Morris stops.

"That's it," he says, "That's the one!"

"How do you know it's him?" I ask in amazement. "What's his

name?"

"Sperman," says Morris. "His name is Mr. Sperman." In my feeble brain, I translated "Sperman" into "Seaman." Morris knew me by now, and Morris was a gentleman. He didn't get angry, he just told this story to everyone who came into the office and showroom. After getting over my shame, I laughed with the rest of them.

One day, a very important buyer came in from Chicago. He was from a firm by the name of Butler Brothers. They owned something like 500 shops by various names.

Mr. L., the buyer, loved our styles. He also liked me. "Take Roslyn and bring her and the new line to our main buying office in Chicago, and I guarantee a good order," says Mr. L.

Morris fell all over himself, he was so pleased. We were finally making it in the big time. The only problem was that Morris hated to fly, and I had never been in a plane before. We were both scared stiff. But it's all in a day's work, so we went.

Morris kept feeding me martinis, which he also imbibed. I developed a headache, so he gave me some aspirins, which he made me drink with coffee. I then developed a stomach ache. I don't remember the plane ride at all; it was just one painful blur.

When we got off the plane, there was Mr. L. waiting for us in his brand new Caddy, all spiffed out and ready to take us to dinner. Morris, who always looked like he had just slept in his clothes, had bought a new raincoat, very expensive, for the occasion. I was dressed in the latest fashion of the day, with a wide-brimmed straw hat and high heeled shoes, in which I could just about manage to walk. We looked like the perfect garment industry representatives.

We get into the car all smiles, carrying on a titillating conversation, when all of a sudden I begin to feel terribly, terribly nauseous. "Morris," I say very quietly, "Morris, I don't feel good. I have to get out of the car!"

"You're kidding," says Morris.

"I'm not," I say.

"Hold it," says Morris.

"I can't," I say. And with that I throw up all over Mr. L.'s new Caddy, Morris's new raincoat, and my new Lord & Taylor dress paid for by the firm. Mr. L. drives us to our hotel. Mr. L. wants to forget that he has ever met us, but he can't. I have left an indelible mark on him and his new Caddy. Mr. L. goes home to his wife.

We have an appointment with him and his merchandise manager at 10:30 the next morning to show our new line. The samples were to have been delivered to our hotel from the airport, but when we arrived there, the samples had unfortunately arrived in Detroit.

Morris stayed up all night waiting for them to be rerouted. I slept fitfully. In the morning, Morris takes me to a very swanky dress shop in the hotel and buys me a new dress and buys himself another raincoat, definitely not as expensive as before. We take our samples in hand, hail a cab, and are off to see Mr. L. and his boss. We arrive all smiles and in good humor, on the outside anyway.

Mr. L. kisses my hand after our very successful meeting and tells me that he will always be thinking of me, especially, he says, when he is driving his Caddy.

"Don't let it bother you," I tell him. "It's all in a day's work."

Fish Like Bubbe Used to Make

This is one of the very few stories about my life that I've ever told in the third person. I thought it would have more of a universal feel for little children that way. Sure enough, it does. On hearing this story, many kids start to noodge their parents to also get a live fish, because it would be the greatest thing to have it swim in the bathtub. But they don't want to eat it either.

-RBP

Not so long ago, two little boys whose names were Martin and Bobby lived near a park called Van Cortlandt Park in the Bronx, in the city of New York. The park was very beautiful and great fun for children. It had a playground on the outside, wonderful paths to walk on, and a lovely little lake right in the middle, where ducks and geese swam. Sometimes the little boys went fishing there. They never caught any fish, only weeds, but they enjoyed it just the same. In the winter, when the lake was frozen, their father would take them ice skating on the lake. They loved their neighborhood and thought it was the best place in the world to live.

There was another reason they loved to live there, and that was because they had their grandma and grandpa living right down the street from them. They loved visiting their bubbe and zayde—that's the Yiddish name for grandma and grandpa—because they would always get something good to eat, like *mandel brot*, a kind of dry pastry with lots of nuts in it, or delicious chicken soup with matzo balls. They were a Jewish family that spoke both Yiddish and English, and their bubbe cooked wonderful Jewish dishes.

Another reason they liked to visit their grandparents was because their zayde would tell them all kinds of stories of what happened long ago. Several days before Rosh Hashana, the Jewish New Year, their zayde told them how hard their bubbe used to work to prepare for the holiday.

"Not like today," he said. "Today, all Bubbe does is go to the supermarket and buy jars of *gefilte* fish. Long ago, she used to go to the fish store where they sold live carp a day or two before Rosh Hashana. Then she would put the fish in the bathtub where they would swim around until she was ready for making the fish. Of course, she had to kill them first, but the fish didn't really mind. They knew it was a holiday, and they knew the Jewish people ate gefilte fish on holidays. The fish were very friendly to the Jews."

Marty and Bobby laughed and laughed because they knew their zayde always said the funniest things. But they loved his stories, and they would repeat them to each other over and over again.

A few days before Rosh Hashana, the two little boys asked their mother if she could make gefilte fish just like Bubbe used to do.

"Of course," said their mother, "but you have to have live fish to do that, and there are so few stores that still sell live fish today."

However, the children pleaded and pleaded with her. "Please, please," they said, "buy some live fish so we can also see them swimming in the bathtub just as you did when you were a kid. Zayde said that you had lots of fun watching them, so you can't say no."

Well, their mother could not talk them out of it and sure enough, just two days before the holiday, their father and mother took their car and drove down to the Lower East Side of Manhattan, where they found a fish store that still sold live carp. They picked out two frisky fellows, put them in a large bucket with water, and drove all the way back to their home in the Bronx. They put the fish into the bathtub. The fish had a grand time swimming back and forth and back and forth in the bathtub, much to the delight of the children, who named one Carpy and the other Joe.

Marty and Bobby loved watching the fish swim. They kept feeding them bread crumbs and any other food they could find, until their mother scolded them and told them that they were stuffing up the water so that the fish would not be able to breathe.

Then they wouldn't come out of the bathroom, even when someone had to go on the toilet. They insisted on eating their lunch in the bathroom, and they even wanted to take their bath with the fish, but they decided against this when their dad told them that the soap would be very bad for the fish. Their mom and dad had a very big job taking out the fish and putting them into a pail every time someone wanted to bathe.

Finally the day came when the fish had to be made into gefilte fish. "Now," said their mom, "we have to kill them and skin them so we can chop them up."

Both children began to cry hysterically. They cried and cried and wouldn't let their mother come near the fish. Marty, who was the older one, said through his sobs, "Rosh Hashana is supposed to be a holiday for kindness and love, and so you don't chop up someone you love." Bobby just stood there, his face wet with tears, shaking his head in agreement with his brother.

""Well," said their mother, "we can't keep the fish in the bathtub forever, even if we don't make them into gefilte fish. What are we going to do with them?"

Bobby suggested they take the fish and put them into the little lake in the park, but Marty said the place for the fish was the Hudson River, because, he said, "Zayde once told me a story about how he caught hundreds and hundreds of fish in the Hudson River."

Their mother smiled and said, "Do you believe everything Zayde tells you?" Both little boys didn't know what to say, because they loved their zayde so.

"Well, we can't do anything today," said their mom. "I'm much too busy preparing for the holiday. We will just have to have those miserable fish for another two days."

"That's great," said their father. "We can take them along with us when we go for *tashlikh*." *Tashlikh* is a ritual that involves going to a flowing body of water to cast off your sins, ask for forgiveness, and say a prayer so you can start with a clean slate for the new year. "We usually throw bread crumbs into the river, but this time, we will throw in the fish to carry away our sins," said their father.

The children didn't like the idea of giving their sins to the fish, but their mother said, "That's enough. Now we have to go to the supermarket to buy a couple of jars of gefilte fish for the holiday.

"You know, children," she added, "even though the fish is in a jar already prepared, once upon a time, they were alive." But Bobby said that was all right, because he didn't know them, and they didn't have a name.

And so, on the second day of Rosh Hoshana, when Jews the

world over go to a flowing body of water to cast away their sins, two not so frisky carp were thrown into the Hudson River. They didn't seem to mind about the sins. They swam happily away.

And never again did those two little boys want their mother to make gefilte fish like Bubbe used to make.

Der Signal: The Transmogrification of a Story

The book that traveled with me from one continent to another, from one generation to another, demonstrates the power of a story, and what it can mean to a family that makes it come alive. To this day, my granddaughter, the composer's daughter, gets the biggest kick out of hearing it. I'm glad I'm still around to see her child enjoy it, too. *-RBP*

In the late 1920s, when I was not quite five years old, my mother started to read to me from a book put out by the Labor Bund that contained many idealistic and educational stories. The Jewish folk schools at that particular time in White Russia were very interested in exposing children to information and learning of a secular nature, rather than dwelling on purely religious themes, which had previously been the norm. This was a society on the cusp of change, and though the books reflected traditional Jewish values, their aim was to broaden the horizons of the young.

My father left for America when I was six months old, leaving my mother and me in our small town. It took over six-and-a-half years for him to become a citizen and accumulate enough money to send for us. This gave my mother a great deal of time to share with me. My mother loved to read, and she started reading stories to me at a very early age. Though some of what she read was way beyond my comprehension, I somehow loved hearing her read them. It wasn't until I heard her read *Der Signal*, a tale by Russian writer Vsevelod Gorschin, that I became aware of being entirely caught up in the action of a story. I was completely focused on what was happening and what the railroad watchman, Semyon, was feeling. I loved the story; I felt fear, dread, exaltation and admiration.

The story was about a railroad watchman who sees a man stealing spikes from the railroad ties. He tries to catch him, but the man gets away. Semyon doesn't know what to do, because a train is coming. He doesn't have a red flag or a crowbar with him; they are in the toolshed. He knows he has to save the people on the train, working people, children. But the shed is too far away. So he picks up a stick, and he takes a knife from out of his boot, and he cuts into the upper part of his arm. Then he takes a handkerchief from out of his pocket, wets it with his blood, and ties it onto the stick, waving it in front of the train. Just as he has gotten the attention of the engineer, he falls down in a faint.

I always asked my mother if Semyon just fainted, or he died. And my mother said, "Well, he just fainted." But somehow I knew in my heart of hearts that Semyon died trying to save all the people on the train.

I had my mother read the story over and over to me until I knew it by heart. When my mother and I finally left for America, I insisted we take the book with us. I could not be parted from the story.

My arrival in America brought a whole new world into being, a world of unfamiliar faces, a less-than-friendly environment with a strange language, the city streets of New York instead of the green meadows of my old home. I had also lost my place in the sun, where I was the central focus of a large and loving extended family. I yearned for the safety and warmth I had known and lost. The railroad watchman Semyon could no longer save the train from derailing.

I put my Yiddish storybook away, wrapped in a paper bag, and faced the realities of a new life in America without my friends. I did not think of Semyon for many years, although I always made sure the storybook was in my possession through the many phases of my life. However, when my two boys reached the age when listening to stories was their greatest pleasure, I remembered my brave old friend, took down my childhood book, dusted off the years of neglect, and painfully began to translate the story into English. My children's reaction to the story was predictable: they loved it. Then again the book was wrapped in its old paper bag, and this time, also put into a plastic envelope for safe-keeping, as its pages were now yellow and brittle with age.

Again it was put in a safe place on the top shelf in a closet and forgotten.

But was it? How fast the years fly in retrospect. My sixtieth birthday was approaching. My oldest son, who is a composer and professor of music, invited me to a concert at Lincoln Center, at which the premiere performance of a new composition he had written was to be played.

"Take Bubbe and the whole family with you," he said. "I think they will all like the piece." And so I did.

Arriving at the concert hall, I am handed a program booklet. I am too excited greeting all the people I meet there to look at the program. The lights start to flicker, summoning all to their seats. We all sit down. The orchestra is quietly waiting for the arrival of the conductor. But instead of the conductor, my mother's voice is heard loud and clear in the hall over the loudspeaker. She is again reading to all the story of Semyon, the railroad watchman, in Yiddish.

I look in amazement at my mother, who is sitting next to me. But she only smiles. She looks like the cat who swallowed the canary. I have no time to question her, as the music begins with the distant sound of a train whistle.

My son had written what he called a secular cantata based on the story *Der Signal* as a birthday present to me. The music was contemporary. The lyrics were in three languages, Russian, Yiddish and English, sung by three young women, with my eighty-two-year-old mother narrating the story in Yiddish on a pre-recorded tape.

I was too stunned to really absorb what was happening, and I could not get over the effort and activity that had gone on behind my back. At intermission, I finally had the opportunity to examine the program, and I saw to my delight that not only had my son written the music to this cherished story, but my daughter-in-law, who is a visual artist, had illustrated it. There were also three printed texts to the story: English, which I had written, Yiddish, taken from the book, and the original Russian, translated from the Yiddish by a colleague of my son's.

The story had indeed traveled far from home, but that is not the end. I'm happy to tell you that I have another son, Bobby, who, with his wife, is involved in theater and puppetry. Since the reaction to Martin's composition was so favorable and since the story itself has a kind of drama and action which made for exciting theater, they decided to mount a shadow puppet show of it, using Martin's music and the taped narration of my mother, who will now forever be heard reading the story.

And so the lovely visual and musical version of *Der Signal* came into being. It is loved by all who see and hear it, and for good reason. But not as good, I must say, as the reasons it is loved by me.

Leonard Bernstein and the Senior Citizens

This story is what might be called a winner. Everyone loves it. One day I get a call from a friend of mine who tells me that one of the producers of National Public Radio would like me to record it for the popular "All Things Considered" program. I am thrilled. I go to the radio station and record it.

Then I wait to hear it on the radio. On the anniversary of Bernstein's death, I hear my story being played. It's me all right, but the story is only about half of what I had recorded, intersected with the music of Brahms' Fourth Symphony.

Several months later at a storytelling conference where I was asked to tell the story, a young storyteller comes up to me and says, "You said that the story you told was your own, but you must have heard it on 'All Things Considered,' as I did.

"I did hear it on the radio," I said, "but it was I who told it."

In amazement she asked, "But how did you get the New York Philharmonic to accompany you?"

"Brains," I said, pointing to my behind. -RBP

My friend Rose was the director of the Andrew Stein Senior Citizen Center on 29th Street in Manhattan. Andrew Stein was then the president of the New York City Council, and the center was one of his pet projects. So with a little word here, and a little word there, the good people of that center got to go to places that would have taken other centers years to arrange.

One day my friend calls and asks me if I would like to go to Lincoln Center to hear Leonard Bernstein conduct the New York Philharmonic Orchestra. It's on a Thursday morning when the public can buy inexpensive tickets to sit in on their rehearsal for the concert that will take place that night. There is only one rub. I will have to come to the senior center first, as she needs assistance with the seniors who will be going there as well.

I have heard many stories about those seniors from my friend Rose to make me hesitate to accept this generous offer. The population of the center consists of a majority of Jews, mixed with Irish, Polish, Italian, Spanish, and African-American seniors, most of whom are over seventy, most of them with minds of their own and the ability to express them, clearly, loudly and with heat. But my friend urges me, telling me that I'll be missing a rare opportunity of hearing Leonard Bernstein for no money down. How could I resist?

I have to arrive at the center at the ungodly hour of seven-thirty a.m.; the rehearsal starts at ten. We have to be seated in Avery Fisher Hall by nine-thirty. The buses that are to take the seniors there are scheduled to leave at eight-forty-five. They have not yet arrived, but the seniors have. Afraid that they will perhaps be late, they come one hour earlier than they have to. They are milling around, getting in the way of the people who are preparing the little brown bags that hold their lunch, which consists of a sandwich—tuna, chicken, or ham and cheese and an apple.

There is a discussion whether to take all the sandwiches in one box and give them out in the bus after the concert, or give them out now and let each of the seniors carry their own. The seniors all make their preference known; they want their bags now! They are worried that they may not get the sandwich of their choice on the bus. "You know," says one little old Jewish women, "we Jews don't eat ham, especially with cheese." They are all given their bags now. What a mistake!

The buses arrive; the seniors, tired from the long wait, gratefully settle down in their seats. When we arrive, a few complain that the ride is too short; they would have liked to sit a little longer on the bus. We all get off at the plaza and enter Avery Fisher Hall. All are duly impressed. Very few of them have ever been here before. They are led down the center aisle by the usher to the best seats in the house, right in the first four rows. They sit there clutching their little brown paper bags, unusually quiet. They observe everything, the orchestra tuning up, the people coming in, the lights, the balconies, the coming and going of the ushers.

Suddenly all is quiet; the concert master has arrived on the stage. He puts his violin under his chin, and the orchestra check their instruments. All are waiting for the entrance of Leonard Bernstein. There is a look of visible anticipation on the faces of the seniors. They have heard so much about this man, and now they will actually see him in person.

Leonard Bernstein enters with his usual flair. He nods to the orchestra and walks to center stage. Facing the audience, he bows to their applause and then addresses them.

"Good morning, ladies and gentlemen," says Bernstein. "Welcome to this morning's rehearsal, I hope you will enjoy the music. However, remember this is a working rehearsal, and we need absolute quiet." He smiles a welcoming smile as he looks down at the first four rows of seniors, turns towards the orchestra, taps his baton on the podium and the music begins.

Not two bars of music had sounded when all over the hall is heard the sound of paper crackling. At first it's just one crackle, but within a few minutes several more sounds follow. They are loud and insistent. Bernstein turns his head away from the orchestra, looks down at the seniors disapprovingly, turns back and continues conducting. The crackling stops. However, it doesn't take long for it to begin again with renewed vigor, and this time it is accompanied by a definite smell of tuna fish.

Bernstein taps the podium with his baton; the orchestra stops playing. He walks over to the edge of the stage and looks directly at the seniors. "I know it's after ten," he says "and you must be hungry. But you can't eat here. Please take those little bags you all seem to be carrying and put them under your seats. During intermission you can eat in the lobby. You must be very quiet here, because any little noise disturbs the musicians, and this hall is designed for sound to be magnified." He waits—the seniors all put their bags under their seats. They smile, a little embarrassed. He nods approval and returns to the podium. The music begins again. I look at my friend Rose, who has slid all the way down in her seat and looks as if she wants to die, right here and now. The music continues, beautifully and emotionally. It's the Brahms Fourth Symphony, and I am lost in it.

Suddenly I hear a muffled sound behind me. I turn and see one of our older men trying to go past the others to the aisle. He has to go to the john, but he is being very polite. He says "Excuse me" to everyone he passes. The other men know where he is going and are triggered to follow for the same reason. They also stand up and start to leave. Bernstein stops the music.

Bernstein is now angry, but he tries to control it. He again walks to the edge of the stage. He takes a deep breath. "Couldn't you wait?" he asks the man already in the aisle. The poor man shrugs his shoulders and puts his hands out in a gesture that says, "What can I do?" He looks like a little kid being caught at something he shouldn't be doing, and Bernstein has to smile in spite of himself. "Okay," he says. "Everyone who has to go to the bathroom go now; we'll wait." The whole audience breaks into laughter, and the New York Philharmonic waits.

The men return. It really took less time than we envisioned, but to us in charge, it seemed like hours. The men sit down. The hall becomes very still. Mr. Bernstein again addresses the seniors. "How many of you belonged to a union?" he asks them. Many hands go up. "These musicians," he says pointing to the orchestra, "also belong to a union. If we do not finish this rehearsal on time, it will cost the Philharmonic time-and-a- half for overtime. The New York Philhamonic cannot afford to pay time-and-a-half for overtime. So, do you think you could be very still and not do anything but listen to the music until intermission?" He asks this with a plea in his voice. The seniors nodded their heads enthusiastically. Leonard Bernstein goes back to his music.

Intermission has mercifully arrived. Mr. Bernstein comes over to the edge of the stage again and quietly asks for the person in charge. My friend Rose walks over to him. Mr. Bernstein gives her a patronizing smile. "I love them," he says. "They're like my own family. But do me a favor and don't bring them here again!"

My friend's answer: "You can count on it!"

The seniors go back to their buses during intermission. They are hungry (they haven't eaten since about six o'clock in the morning), they are tired, and they really have had enough of culture. They eat their sandwiches on the bus and finish them off with juice that was held for them there—thank God.

Riding back to the center to be dismissed, they talk about the concert, about the concert hall, about Leonard Bernstein. "Isn't he wonderful?" says a chubby Jewish lady to her friend. "And to think he's one of ours. He's such a *mensch*."

"What's a mensch?" asks an African-American women sitting on the other side of her.

"Oh," says the Jewish woman, "A mensch is a fine person who doesn't only think of himself, who knows about a lot of things and cares about people."

"Well," says her black friend, "If he's a mensch, then he's one of ours, too!"

And so are we all.

On the Subway from the Bronx

I told this story to a tough, all-male high school class. At first, they were not too sure they were going to listen to this white, chubby old lady. But with each story I told, I could feel them become more and more interested. They began to make comments about the various happenings and misadventures. This subway story was last. The period was over, and as they passed by me to go out, many of them shook my hand and said with laughter, "Goodbye, Mrs. P-E-R-R-Y. Have a good day." For me, their response was better than a bouquet of roses. *-RBP*

It happened in New York City, on the subway from the Bronx to Manhattan one morning at 10 a.m., to be exact, on my way to work. Sitting lost in the process of going over a story I had written which lay opened on my lap, I was suddenly jolted by the loud and raucous voices of children coming into my car. A fourth-grade class was going on a field trip. The children were of an ethnic and racial mix that could only be found in the city of New York. To me they were all a pain in the neck, and I tried to ignore the youthful exuberance and shut my mind and eyes to the excitement and laughter. I had to go over this story! This very evening was to be my first professional storytelling performance. I was finally going to get paid for performing. Although I had told this particular story many times before, it now occurred to me that I didn't remember a single word of it.

Suddenly I had the distinct feeling that someone or something was breathing down my neck. Opening my eyes, I found the body of a small Chinese boy almost in my lap. He was trying to read the title of the story I was holding, and he was having a difficult time of it. Looking at his soft, round cheek so close to mine, seeing his childish lips trying to form the words, I experienced a feeling of tender affection, and I asked, "Having trouble?"

Sheepishly he raised his shoulders and nodded his head yes. "Of course you are," I said smiling. "It's no wonder, because although the letters are English, the words are in a foreign language. Do you want me to read them to you?" He nodded again. And so I read, '*Mein bubbe Shayne hut mir kayn mol nisht lieb gehat.* That's a language called Yiddish," I said. "It was spoken by a lot of Jewish people in the little Russian town where I was born. It means, 'My grandmother, whose name was Shaine, never liked me.'"

The children standing around us smiled. "Why didn't she like you?" asked a smart-alecky kind of kid with a wicked grin.

"Yeah," said his friend, a black boy with a face so handsome, it was hard to stop staring at him. "Yeah, why didn't she like you?"

"Oh, it's a long story," I answered, thinking that would be the end of that. But it wasn't. It was only the beginning.

"Did you write the story yourself and is it about you?" asked a Latino-looking youngster, who had by now somehow managed to squeeze himself in between me and the passenger sitting next to me.

"Yes," I said. "I wrote it, and I'm going to tell it to a lot of people tonight." The minute that sentence was out of my mouth, I realized it was the wrong thing to say, because the response was inevitable.

"Can you tell it to us?" asked a shy friend of the Chinese boy, whose Asian origin was difficult for me to place.

"Well, I don't know," I said. "The subway is really no place to tell stories."

"Why not?" asked the Latino-looking kid.

"Because it's noisy and crowded and people will think I'm crazy," I answered, looking for logic. But it didn't seem logical to them. They sensed that I was vacillating.

"Aw, come on," they said. "We want to hear the story."

How could I refuse such an eager audience? And anyway, what was more important, the story or my dignity?

At my age, dignity takes second place. And so I began to give them an introduction to the story. "Well, the story is about a little Jewish girl who lived in a small town in Russia. It's about how unhappy she was when she had to leave her family and friends to come to America. You see, she couldn't speak English when she came here. And so she had a hard time making new friends, which made her miss her old home."

I seemed to have struck a magic chord, because the children all started talking at once. They, too, had come from another country. They, too, had difficulty learning English. But now they assured me they had lots of friends. The Chinese boy told us he came from Hong Kong, and at first all the English he knew was how to say, "Yes."

"How do you say 'yes' in Chinese?" I asked him.

"Sheh, sheh," he answered.

This started a discussion on how to say *yes* in the various languages of the children around me. The friend of the Chinese boy, who turned out to be Korean, said his word for *yes* was *nay*. My Spanish friend sitting at my right told us with pride that he came from Puerto Rico, and he says *si*.

The handsome black boy, not wanting to be left out, said he came from the South, and he says, "Yes."

"What part of the South?" I asked him. He shrugged his shoulders. This evoked a comment by the original smart-aleck that our Southerner really came from the South Bronx.

"Where do you come from, wise guy?" I retorted.

Putting his hands on his hips and throwing his shoulders back, he announced with both pride and defiance that he came from New York, New York. And he says *yeah*!

This elicited peals of laughter from the children, who had by now become a large group, all crowding around and wanting to be part of the fun.

The Chinese boy, however, was not going to let me divert him from his original quest. "Tell us the story," he said.

"Yes, yes," pleaded the children all together, "Tell us the story."

In a loud voice, which had to overcome the clatter of the train, I told them about the loneliness of mothers, wives and children whose sons, husbands and fathers left for America to look for a new and better life. I told them about the father of the little girl who went to America and wrote letters and sent money to his wife and child who had remained in the old country without him, but who forgot that his mother missed him, too. So my grandmother was jealous of my mother, and my mother was not very nice to my grandmother. And so my grandmother, whose name was Shaine, thought I was like my mother, and that was why she didn't like me. The children all thought that was unfair. But I assured them that I took measures to change all that.

This sparked a reply from a blonde little girl who told us that her mother and grandmother never fight, but her mother and father fight all the time. One after another the children shared a little of their lives with us. I felt moved by their intense listening to each other, and their bright comments presented me with a gift of being part of a shared experience.

We were so engrossed in our conversation that the teacher of the children had a hard time getting their attention. "We must get off at the next station, which is Fifty-ninth Street," she shouted. "Please get ready."

"Do you come to schools and tell stories?" they asked me hurriedly. And without waiting for a reply shouted, "What's your name, what's your name?"

"Mrs. Perry," I shouted back as they turned to go. And as they did not seem to hear me, I spelled it out for them. "P-E-R-R-Y," I said.

"Good-bye, Mrs. P-E-R-R-Y," they shouted as they noisily left the car.

How silent it seemed without them. Hesitantly I looked around and saw, to my amazement, a solid row of smiles on the faces of the other passengers who had been listening to our conversation.

I left the subway at Thirty-fourth Street and walked as if in a trance into my office.

"You'll never guess what happened to me on the subway," I said to my associates.

In unison, they all answered, "You were mugged!"

"No," I replied, still in that warm place of children, noise and graffiti. "No," I repeated. "Not mugged—loved!

I'm from New Haven

If someone had told me this story about this woman, I would not have believed it—she was such an unusual woman, and her story was so very strange. *-RBP*

I recently wrote a story called "On the Subway from the Bronx" and told it to a group of women in charge of developing multicultural activities for a cooperative housing development, which not too many years earlier had been overwhelmingly Jewish. Now, there was a mix of many ethnic groups that were unaccustomed to cooperative living. The aim of the activities was to acquaint the new coop owners with the diversity of the people who lived in their midst. The women felt the story I had told them would make a perfect flyer to introduce the residents to their project. They planned to put the flyers under everyone's door.

The story was too long for a one-page flyer, and they asked me if I could shorten it to fit the paper. The day was Friday, and they had to have the condensed version by Monday. I had a date to spend the weekend with my children in New Haven, but I said yes to their request, as it takes two hours to get from New York to New Haven. I knew I could accomplish the task in that period of time. I was too tired going there, but I knew I could do it on my way home.

Going back home, I arrive at the New Haven railroad station early to make sure I would be one of the first on the train to get a seat by the window. I take out my pad, pen, and a copy of my story and start to work. The train fills up with people; no one sits next to me. I am grateful for that, as it gives me more room and less of a distraction. I am the only one sitting by myself.

As the train starts to pull out of the station, there appears a very, very large women carrying many packages. She is all flustered, talking to herself about how crowded the train is, and that there is so little room for packages, and all the seats are taken. She then sees the empty seat next to me, and she proceeds to put all her things overhead, some of which fall to the floor and have to be rearranged to fit into the space. Tears are running down her cheeks as she sits down with a great sigh, wiping her eyes. Not wanting to appear heartless, I make the mistake of giving her a sympathetic smile. That was all I had to do to start her talking to me non-stop.

"I'm from New Haven," she says, now really starting to cry. "I don't know if you saw all the people that came to see me off. I hated to leave, because I love New Haven, and I love my family. But I have to go back to South Carolina, where my husband is.

"I hate my husband's family. They are so unfriendly, so mean. They don't even call me by my name; they just call me 'John's wife.' They don't accept me because I'm from the North. I wouldn't go back there, but we have a pretty good business, an appliance store. I can't afford to leave it. It's not that I'm so crazy about John. You know, he used to beat me, until I got smart and gave him one good shove which knocked him against the far wall. After that he kept his hands to himself. Another reason I hate to go back is that I'm so afraid of riding on trains."

"If you hate riding on trains, why don't you fly? I ask her.

"I hate flying even worse. What I would like to do would be to drive back."

"It's such a long trip, and it's so boring," I say.

"Oh no," she says, " I love to drive, and I wouldn't find it boring at all. You see, I drive all the time; that's my job."

"You're a taxi driver?"

"No, I'm a truck driver. I have a helper, and I deliver the appliances to our customers."

"You mean you actually help carry things like refrigerators and air conditioners?"

"What do you mean 'help'? My helper helps me. It's not hard if you know how to do it."

She now begins to tell how she does it, when I politely tell her to excuse me for not listening, as I have work to do before I get to New York. She nods her head sadly and stops talking. I start my writing.

It doesn't take long before I feel her hand on mine. "Excuse me," she says, "but we are coming to a bridge, and I'm terrified crossing a bridge by train. Could I please hold your hand when we cross it?"

I look at this enormous woman frightened like a child, and something in me wants to help her. Oh well, I think to myself, I'll just have to work on this paper tonight.

"Okay," I say, "just take my hand, close your eyes, and I'm going to tell you the story I was going to write about." I start to tell her the story of "On the Subway from the Bronx."

She listens with an intensity that reminds me of children completely enraptured by the storyteller. Her eyes remain closed throughout the rather long tale.

We are approaching New York when I end the story and tell her to open her eyes, that all is well, and I am almost home.

She has a surprised look on her face. "You mean we crossed the bridge and we are already near New York?"

"Yes," I say.

"Oh, that story was so wonderful," she says, "I could actually see those children on the subway talking to you, and you answering them, and all the people looking at you."

I smile at her. "Good," I say, as I start gathering my things to leave. She grabs my hand again and begins to cry. "Why are you crying now?" I ask her.

"This is the first time in my whole life that someone told me a story that was just for me." She buries her face in her handkerchief, and I gently remove my hand.

Crossing Fifth Avenue

I've told this story to many people, but never onstage. Believe it or not, what I've put down here is the upbeat part of the story. What happened after this incident is a nightmare that could only have occurred in a country with no universal healthcare. Medicare refused to cover me because it was an accident; the taxi company refused to give me the name of their insurer; the police department insisted that I go down to the station and pay $10 for the accident report. Meanwhile, my blood pressure was skyrocketing, my back and head were killing me, and I had no idea how I was going to get to a doctor.

-RBP

The afternoon was balmy, early autumn. I was returning from conducting an all-day workshop and storytelling performance, and I was paid in cash. I usually don't like to walk around the city with that amount of money in my bag, but I was going to a memorial service for my friend Ruth Rubin, who had recently died, and there was no time for anything else but to get there. I was already late.

My mood bordered on the dark side. Ruth Rubin, that wonderful folklorist, singer, social activist, author and teacher was no more. It was true; she had been an old lady in her late eighties and in a state of early dementia, but what a sad ending to such an illustrious life. As she aged, very few people came to visit. She died alone, without the applause and the admiring throngs that had defined her life.

When I arrived at the hall where the event was taking place, I was shocked at the crowds milling around the door trying to get in. The place was packed. Suddenly, Steve Zeitlin, a folklorist friend of mine who had organized the memorial service, came out to address the overflow crowd. After telling us they had installed a loud speaker outside so the speeches would be heard, he sees me standing there and pulls me in to the hall.

I am overcome with resentment. "Look at that crowd," I say.

"When she was alive, no one came to see her and now, everyone is going to say how wonderful she was, but she won't hear it. How unfair it all is."

"Steve," I suddenly say with honest emotion, "I want you to make me my memorial while I'm still alive." Steve laughs and assures me that he will certainly do it, but I have to tell him when I plan to depart.

The speeches were moving and the deference and admiration for her life and her work were beautifully enunciated, but the overall sadness does not leave me. When another friend suggests that I accompany her to her car, and she will take me to my home, I graciously refuse.

"I prefer to walk," I say. "It's not far, and it will do me good." And that's how I come to be crossing Fifth Avenue.

Standing on the corner waiting for the light to change, Ruth is still on my mind. As I enter the walkway to cross the street, I see through the corner of my eye a taxi making a left turn onto Fifth Avenue, and he is heading directly towards me at top speed. In fact, he is going so fast he can't stop the car even though he sees me. He turns the cab sharply to the right trying to avoid me, and he succeeds in not hitting me full force. But he swipes me, knocking me forcefully down into the middle of the street.

It's strange how the mind works. When I saw him coming toward me I raised my hands as if to stop him. I knew he was going to hit me, and in that instant I said to myself, "Well, here it is, I'm done for. It's a shame I'm going to miss my memorial."

I hit the pavement hard with the back of my head and the lower part of my back. I am sure my head is split in half; the pain is so extreme. My pocketbook flies into the air, and one shoe falls off.

The taxi driver jumps out of his cab, almost as distraught as I am. He is a very young man with a foreign accent. He keeps repeating over and over again as he bends over me that he is so sorry and am I all right?

"Why were you going so fast?" I ask him in between moans of pain. "You shouldn't have been driving so fast!"

He looks so upset that I try to make him feel better. "Don't worry," I say, "I'm not dead yet." Strange as it seems, I actually feel sorry for him. What the hell is the matter with me? I think. He almost killed me, and here I am worrying about him.

In the twinkling of an eye, a crowd gathers around me, all wanting to help. Through my pain, I hear people shouting for someone to call an ambulance, the police, and maybe was there a doctor in the crowd?

Instead of a doctor, a middle-aged women comes over to me and puts the *New York Times* under my head. It is Sunday, and I recognize the paper by its size. It doesn't help much. She then asks me if I am cold. I groan a painful yes, and before I know what is happening, she takes off her coat and covers me with it.

Suddenly I hear the sound of a fire engine heading straight towards me at top speed. Now I think I'm really a goner. It is already dark, and they'll never see me lying in the middle of the street and will run right over me. But the shrill siren stops, and a fireman runs over to me.

"Why did you come?" I ask him. "I'm not on fire."

"You don't have to be on fire for us to help you," he says. "Don't move—we are going to put a brace on your neck in case of a break."

While he is doing this, the woman who gave me the coat comes over to me and asks if I want her to call somebody at home. I start to tell her my number, when a policeman appears.

"Don't give anyone your number," he says. "I'll take care of it."

"But she gave me her coat," I say.

And then I remember my pocketbook with all my money in it. "My bag," I moan, "my bag, can I have my bag?"

The woman goes to get my bag, but the policeman stops her. "We'll take care of your bag," he says, as he takes it away from her.

"No, no," I cry, "that's just what I'm afraid of. I want my bag."

The policeman brings me my bag and puts it on my chest as if I had just given birth to it. He shoves the women aside, and I decide that I don't like him very much.

The ambulance arrives. Two paramedics jump out and start questioning me. Can I move my toes? Do I see how many fingers they are holding up? What's my name? What's the name of the president of the United States?

"What?" I say "At a time like this you want me to worry about who the hell is president of the United States? My head is killing me, and you want to talk politics?"

"With your attitude, you're going to be okay," one of them says. "How's the back?"

"Hurting a lot, but not as bad as the head."

"Any blood?" the other one asks the fireman.

"I don't think so, but you should try the neck to make sure it's not broken."

Oh my God, I think, a broken neck. Here goes my career.

The two men take off the neck brace and start to gently move my head. "Doesn't look like it," they both agree.

"We are going to put you on a stretcher. Now just lay still, and we'll try not to hurt you. Give that pocketbook you're clutching to the policeman so we can strap you in."

"Oh no you don't," I say still holding on tightly to my bag, "You can strap me in just as I am. And while you're at it, don't forget my shoe." They shake their heads in resignation and do so.

I'm super uncomfortable on the stretcher. I feel as though I'm falling off to one side, and it hurts my back.

"The stretcher is killing my back, and I'm going to fall off," I say.

"Sweetheart," says one of the paramedics, in an exasperated voice, "you have never been so safe in your life. And by the way, what hospital do you want us to take you to?"

"You mean I have a choice?" I can't believe what I hear. My head feels like it's going to explode any minute, my back is a sheath of pain, and I am given options on New York City hospitals.

"I want to go to the nearest hospital to where we are."

"You can go to Bellevue or St. Vincent's."

"I'll take St. Vincent's, it's closer."

"If you say so," he answers me. I am not reassured.

The ambulance starts going with its sirens blaring, bouncing over the many potholes so endemic to our New York City streets. One of the young men takes my pulse, then my blood pressure. I see by the look on his face that all is not well. He waits a minute and then takes my pressure again, then again and again and again. He leaves my side and starts to talk on the phone to what I presume is someone at the hospital. He speaks as quietly as he can, but I hear the number two hundred and sixty-three.

He comes back and takes my pressure again. "I have a blood pressure of two hundred and sixty three, don't I?"

"What makes you say that?"

"I heard you on the phone."

"You weren't supposed to hear." With that remark, he puts an oxygen mask over my nose.

"I'm going to die, or at least have a stroke," I say through the mask. And for the first time he smiles and says, "Oh no, not you!"

I smile back a pathetic little smile and gratefully sink into oblivion.

The Jews Are Coming, The Jews Are Coming!

This story has become a beloved myth of my friends in the Sindicate. Every time we get together and reminisce, this story comes up, and we laugh just as hysterically as we did when it first happened. -*RBP*

We were a group of women in our early fifties, drawn together by our need for companionship and mutual intellectual pursuits. The women's movement was then in full swing, which gave us permission to band together to follow a dream.

Originally there were six of us, all working women, all with children: Otti from Louisiana who had been Catholic, Presbyterian, and who was now Unitarian married to a Unitarian minister; Irene, Jewish, married, who attended a Conservative or Reform or Reconstructionist synagogue; Jan divorced, Protestant, who was now a free thinker; Shirley, Jewish, married to a Reform rabbi; myself, recently remarried, secular, culturally Jewish; Rose, divorced, once-Jewish, now a practicing Buddhist; and Doris, divorced, Jewish, once secular, now Orthodox. We were later joined by Hilda, who was Lutheran, married to a Lutheran minister.

We were about as diverse as we could be, and we called ourselves the Sindicate, a real-estate term with a spelling change to suit our frame of mind. Our dream was to buy a property in which we could all live together in our old age.

And so every year we left our husbands and children and went looking for our dream house. Our goal was never reached, but in that quest we traveled, had celebrations, adventures and mishaps galore. But the greatest thing of all was that we formed a bond that gave us comfort through many of the trials and tribulations of our lives and it has remained so to this day.

We had already visited many parts of the United States, where the climate was either too hot or cold, rainy or dry, too far away or too near. We tried to avoid Florida, because everyone was moving there. As you can see, we weren't run-of-the-mill women, but when one of us suggested the west coast of Florida, Fort Myers or even Sanibel Island, it seemed acceptable to most of us. However, I pointed out the possibility that there might not be any Jews living there, and although I was as inclusive as they come, not religious, very democratic, I had to have some sprinkling of Jews around.

Irene solved my trepidation by sending away for a telephone book from Fort Myers to see how many Cohens lived there. She said the amount of Cohens would tell us the approximate amount of the Jewish population. She gave me the job of looking it up. Since I'm dyslexic and my spelling ability comes and goes, I somehow spelled Cohen as Coen. There were no Coens in Fort Myers. Everyone thought that was impossible; there were Cohens all over the world; why not in Fort Myers? They took the telephone book away from me and found the right amount of Cohens to make me feel comfortable, and so we rented an apartment for a week, right on the beach in Sanibel Island, which is connected to Fort Myers by a bridge.

We all met at the Newark Airport in New Jersey at four o'clock, checked our luggage, and sat waiting for our plane, which was to leave at six. It was a cold winter's day, and there had been snow flurries throughout the day. Suddenly the snow started to come down in abundance. There was an announcement that our plane would be delayed. We waited, but in vain, as we were told that the snow would not stop until morning, and all flights are cancelled. We asked about our luggage and were told that we need not worry; our luggage would be at the airport when we arrived there. We all headed for Shirley's house, the nearest one to the airport.

There were not enough beds to accommodate all of us, and so a few of us, the hearty souls, slept on the floor. We were all in good humor when we arrived back at the airport the next day, boarded our plane, and landed in a wet and cloudy Fort Myers. We went for our luggage, but it wasn't there. We were told not to worry, as the luggage would be delivered to our apartment within the hour. We rented a van and headed for Sanibel Island in the rain. The apartment was very nice, comfortable, with enough sleeping space for us all. Some of us went shopping for food and drink in the rain, while the others stayed in the apartment waiting for our suitcases. It never stopped raining, and our luggage never arrived.

We were not daunted by the weather and went looking at available houses in the rain. We saw a few that were out of the question, one or two that had possibilities if we wanted to do a great deal of remodeling. We came back home and argued who would get the corner rooms, where would we put our visiting children if and when they visited, would our husbands go along with our arrangements, and all the while we had a merry time eating and drinking.

And then it happened. The sun peeked out of the clouds and decided to say hello for a moment. Irene and I grabbed our towels and ran down to sit by the pool. Irene took a sun reflector that had been left in the apartment to aid her in getting more sun on her face.

I just sat looking at the water, when a woman joined us. She asked us if we lived in the apartment house. I told her that we only rented an apartment, as we were looking to buy a house.

"Have you seen anything you liked?" she wanted to know. I told her how difficult it was to find a house to suit our purpose. I them told her about our group, which did not want to be separated in our old age, and that was the purpose of our search.

She was very impressed with the whole idea and with us. She then bent closer to me and almost whispered into my ear, "Listen, if you find anything that you think might do, even if you have to do work on it, you better buy it as soon as possible, because the Jews are coming."

"What do you mean, the Jews are coming?" I wanted to know. "What happens when they come? Do prices go up or down, or does something else happen?"

My friend, Irene, is now shifting uncomfortably on her lounge chair. She hates contention, and she is afraid of what I will say. But I really wanted to know. The women continues, "It's not the prices at all. You sound like you come from New York; don't you know about the Jewish women?" And she stops, waiting for me to tell her.

"What about the Jewish women?"

"Why, the Jewish women change their clothes five times a day."

"They do?" I say. "I never noticed. I have lived in New York almost all of my life, and I never noticed that they changed their clothes five times a day. When do they have time to do that, since so many of them are working?"

"Well," she says, a little perturbed. "They do it here."

"And you don't like it? I would absolutely love it! Just think, a fashion show every time you see a Jewish woman. I'm an ethnographer, and it appears to me that we Americans just love to travel, and we just love to learn about other cultures. I am interested in how people live, what they eat, how they dress, and here you have another culture right next door. Learn to enjoy it!"

"Well," says the woman, "I never thought of it that way." Before I could make another comment it starts raining again, and Irene and I start to leave.

"Will you come down again?" she asks me. "It was so nice talking with you."

"I'll try," I say, as Irene and I head for the elevator, where we fall into hysterical laughter. When we open the door to our apartment, Irene bursts into the room, where our friends are lying around eating and drinking as usual.

Irene said, "You should have seen a woman we met by the pool who told Roz, of all people, that the Jews are coming, and that Jewish women change their clothes five times a day."

At which point all of us howled. You see, our luggage never arrived, and we had all been wearing the same clothes for days.

My Sister on the Hood

When my sister told me of her experience with the car, she said, "That's the kind of story you should tell."

So I said I will, and I did. It is one of the few that I tell that I myself did not experience. But although I didn't experience my sister on the hood, I have certainly experienced my sister! -RBP

My sister Phyllis, whose name in Yiddish is Faygele, or little bird, was a very pretty child. Not only was she pretty, but she was also bright and talented. She could sing even as a child, as beautifully as her namesake. She was a delight to all who saw her and heard her. However, Faygele was always in trouble, because she had a definite mind of her own and her very own sense of justice.

Phyllis was the kind of child who, when my mother said, "Faygele, don't touch," touched, because she wanted to find out how it felt. She was the kind of child who, when my mother said, "Faygele, don't go there," went there, because she wanted to find out what was there. This characteristic has stayed with my sister Phyllis to this day, and the story I want to share with you is just one of many incidents in her life that can only have happened to her and only in New York.

My sister is a singer. She sings jazz, she sings the folk songs of other nations, but mostly she sings Yiddish songs. I'm not bragging when I say that she is one of the best in the field. She has, and still does, perform professionally. Why she has not become a well-known celebrity known by millions is material for many other stories. Suffice it to say, those who hear her, love her. She is a featured singer on several recordings with other singers. Her admirers have urged her time and time again to make a recording of her own, and finally, after many years, she agreed to do so.

As I said before, Phyllis has a mind of her own, and so she set out to make this recording exactly as she visualized it. She enlisted first-class musicians and technical people in her project. She selected both Yiddish and English songs, all beautiful, all chosen to communicate emotion and art. But Phyllis did even more. She translated some of the Yiddish songs into English and some of the English songs into Yiddish, so that they could be heard in both languages. That made it very hard for the music arranger, as he did not understand the Yiddish words that had to fit in with the music of the English songs. Another problem was the sheet music for some of the older English songs was very hard to locate. Finally, after much searching, Phyllis found what she was looking for in a music office on Forty-sixth Street. That was where she was going on that fateful morning in February.

There had been a terrible snowstorm the week before, and the streets were covered with ice. My poor sister had had the misfortune of slipping on the ice and splintering the wrist of her right hand. She now had a cast from her elbow to her fingers, but the sheet music had to be delivered to the arranger, who was doing her a favor by giving her his precious time, and he couldn't be held up. So instead of taking public transportation to go to Forty-sixth Street off Sixth Avenue in Manhattan, she jumps in her car and heads downtown.

My sister is very capable, and she drives the car with her left hand, only using the fingers of her right hand for additional support. By some miracle, she arrives on Forty-sixth Street in one piece. But where does one find parking in the city? You don't! So what does she do; she parks at a meter at which parking is not allowed during that time of day. To show her good intentions, to show that she is not trying to get away with anything, she puts a quarter in the meter. Her reasoning is that she will only be there for a minute. She has alerted the receptionist by phone that she will pick up the music, and it should be waiting for her. It is, and she is really there for what seems to her a minute or two. But fate takes a hand!

As she comes out of the building, she sees a towtruck driver putting that infamous hook on her car. She emits an ear-splitting scream to stop the action, but the driver pays no attention. With that, my sister Phyllis takes a leaping dive and jumps on the hood of the car.

The driver can't believe his eyes. "Hey, lady!" he says. "Hey, lady, what the hell are you doing? Lady, get off that hood."

"No," says my sister. "I will not. If you insist on taking my car, you're going to have to take me, too. I was only parked for a minute, and I yelled to you to stop, not to put that hook on, but you didn't pay any attention. What kind of human being are you, anyway? Can't you see I'm in trouble? I have a broken arm; this is my first time out of the house. I haven't got the strength or the money to go to get it back from the pound."

"Tell it to the judge, lady," says the driver. "The law says that once I start taking a car, I can't stop in the middle. So get off!" But my sister remains on the hood.

Meanwhile, a crowd gathers. "Hey, lady," asks one of the men standing by. "Ya wanna cup of coffee while you're waiting?"

"Yes, thanks," says my sister. "Maybe you have a cigarette, too. I'm trying to give up smoking so I don't carry them on me, but I sure need one now."

"Of course," says the man. "Be my guest." He gives her a cigarette and goes for a container of coffee. And now my sister Phyllis sits on the hood of her car smoking a cigarette, drinking coffee, with a cast on her arm and an ever-growing crowd of people on both sides of the street, waiting to see the outcome of one lone woman against the might of the mighty New York City police force.

It doesn't take long for a police car to come screeching up, its sirens blaring. The police first talk to the driver and then approach my sister. One of the officers is a man, the other a woman. The man comes over to my sister.

"Lady," he says, "Ya gotta get off the car, or you'll be in a lot of trouble. You're parked in an illegal spot; it's a tow-away zone, and the driver has to take the car right now. If you don't get off, we'll carry you off."

My sister gives the officer a look of injured innocence. "I can't believe you're talking to me like this," she says. "I will not get off. I was only parked for a minute or two. I came back before he started to attach the car, and I yelled to him not to do it, but he went right along and did it anyway."

"Yeah," say some of the onlookers, "yeah, let her go." The policeman gives them a dirty look.

"Look at me," says my sister, now very agitated. "Look at me; I'm an old woman with white hair and a broken arm. I'm in pain and I'm cold and I can't go on with this." My sister is now talking at the top of her deep, rich contralto voice that can be heard all the way down the next street.

The officer is showing signs of wear, when his female partner comes over. She walks up to my sister, gives her an understanding look, and says, "Madam, calm down; we can't tell the driver to release the car, but we can call our supervisor. He might actually be able to do something. However, you'll have to quiet down."

"I will, I certainly will," says my sister, now speaking in lower tones. "But I'm not getting off the hood. It's not human, and it's not just. Please go and call him."

The young policewoman leaves to make the call. Meanwhile the crowd on both sides of the street grows and grows.

In a short time, another police car arrives with sirens shrieking, lights flashing. There is now a tow truck and two police cars blocking the way. Cars wanting to drive down the street can't pass. The traffic builds, and horns are blaring. The cars extend into Sixth Avenue and are beginning to block the traffic there. More and more people gather.

A sergeant jumps out of the police car and surveys the scene. He goes over to the two officers and confers with them. He then walks over to my sister still sitting on the hood.

"Madam," he says, "Look what you are doing; you are disrupting the whole city. Please get off the hood."

My sister shakes her head with a definite no. Then she takes another tack.

"Look, Sergeant McCarthy," she says, noticing his name on the badge. "I'm a singer. I'm making a recording, and I just ran into this building to get a sheet of music that was being held for me. I need that music very badly. I was only there for a second. As you can see, I have a broken arm and I don't feel well. That's why I took the car."

The sergeant wants to get rid of this whole mess. He looks at my sister; he looks at the traffic jam; he looks at all the people looking at him.

"You know," says my sister in a gentle tone, "the record I'm making is of folk music. It even has one of your folksongs on it." And with that she starts to sing, "Tura lura lural, Tura lura li, Tura lura lural...."

"Okay, okay," says the sergeant, smiling. "But don't you ever park again in a No Parking Zone." And with that, he motions to the driver of the tow truck to remove the hook.

My sister gets off the hood, and the crowd goes wild with cheering and applauding. The little people had won. Everyone went away smiling—except maybe the tow truck driver.

Guess Who's Coming to Seder

I told this story in Oklahoma at the Winter Tales Festival. When the performances were over and the storytellers left the stage to join the audience, a woman came up to me, put her arms around me, and started to cry. She said she was German; she had come to America as an immigrant from Germany, and her in-laws, who were Jewish, absolutely refused to accept her.

She said that when she heard me telling that story, she was deeply moved, reliving her own life and how differently I felt about my daughter-in-law. She said that since I gave her a present, she had to give me a present. "You're going to be here for a while?" she asked. "I'll come right back." In twenty minutes, she returned carrying a package. In the package were two loaves of bread. She told me the bread came from her family bakery, the best bakery in Oklahoma City. She wanted me to have bread, because bread is the soul of life, and, she said, "that's what you gave me—food for the soul."

-RBP

It was a cold and windy Wednesday evening toward the end of March, when the telephone rang in my newly decorated apartment in New York City.

A cheery "Hi Mom," came sparkling across the wires, which connected me to my son, now attending a university in Massachusetts—Harvard! Let me tell you, that boy is the apple of my eye. Tall, handsome, bright as they come, and a mensch, to boot.

"Hello, Billy darling," I say. Is something wrong that you are calling me in the middle of a Wednesday? You always call on the weekend. You're not sick or something?"

"Oh Mom, you're always worrying about me," says Billy in a disgusted voice. "No, I'm not sick; in fact I feel wonderful. I just called to talk over my plans for coming home for Passover. I would like to bring someone home with me for the holiday, and I'd like you to give it some serious thought."

"Since when do I have to have a serious discussion with you about bringing someone home with you? You've been doing it for years."

"This time it's different. She's different," says my son in a tone I don't recognize.

"Are you in love?" I ask. "If you are, of course, bring her. I'm sure we all want to meet her."

"No," says Billy, "I'm not in love. But I like her a lot, and I'd like to bring her home."

"So what is the problem?"

"It's just that she is different," says my Billy, and for the first time in his life, he is at a loss for words.

Fear is now closing in on my senses. How do I really feel about this different girl? This is really a big decision I have to make on the spot. I sit down, my legs buckling. Taking a deep breath, gathering all my so-called idealism, courage, and social consciousness into this reply, I answer him, my heart pounding.

"Listen here, William, I know how hard it is even to have a good, ongoing relationship with someone of your own class, religion, ethnic group. You know how society treats those who go against its rules. You know you are asking for heartache and hardship for the two of you. But I want to tell you something, Bill. I trust you and your ability to choose the right thing for yourself. I know that if you have chosen this girl, she must be someone special and wonderful. It will be rather hard for some people in our family to understand, but as far as I'm concerned, just bring this black girl home, and I will make her most welcome."

"But Ma," Billy wails, "she's not black!"

"She is not black," I repeat uncomprehendingly. "So what is she?"

"She is German. Not Jewish German; she is German German."

"She is German German," I repeat. "Don't you dare bring her! How dare you bring into our house a daughter of the murderers of our people, the murderers of my entire family?"

"Oh Mom," moans my son, "I had an idea you would react this way, but I hoped that your sense of justice and humanity would overcome your outrage. She is as much a victim as anyone. She was born in Hamburg towards the end of the war, and as a baby endured all the terrible bombing of the Allies. She is a wonderful, intelligent, talented and kind person. She feels as heartsick about the Holocaust as any one of us, and you know yourself that all the Germans were not Nazis. I know you would love her if you met her."

"Don't bring her!" I say.

"Mom, I call on your concern for all battered and bruised people. I call on your lovingkindness, and I call on your Jewish consciousness, which understands the suffering of discrimination. I call on your sense of decency and your often repeated avowal of judging people on their own merits, not on their ancestry."

Now I ask you, can anyone resist such an appeal from a beloved son? I had no defense against his pleading, and in spite of everything within me that cried out against the association of my son and this unknown German girl, I consented to her coming.

For the first time in my life, I dreaded the arrival of Passover. Usually this holiday is a most joyous occasion for us. The message of freedom that the Exodus from Egypt inspires has motivated our free-thinking family to make from all our tables one table and from all our songs one song to celebrate this cherished holiday with pride in our own individual sense of being Jewish. But not this year. This year my beloved son was bringing home to us an enemy of our people.

Then, one Sunday morning a few days before Passover, the doorbell rings, and I hurry over to open the door. Looking through the peephole, I see the familiar face of my son, and he seems to be alone. Joy fills my heart as I open the door. Standing before me is the beaming face of my six-foot tall son, and under his arm stands a little girl not five feet tall with big brown eyes and blonde hair pulled back in a flowing ponytail. She stands there visibly shaking with fright.

There we stand, the three of us looking at each other for what seemed an eternity, sorting out the threads of our emotions. The frightened face of the girl conveys more to me than any words could express.

I smile a tight little smile. Her eyes light up, and a sweet expression crosses her pretty face.

A feeling of anguish engulfs me. God in heaven! What do we humans do to one another!

I hold out my hand. "Come here, my enemy," I say. And I envelop her in my arms.

Jack Waldman

This is one of many failed attempts to get me a man. To me, the men my age just seem so unappetizing. To tell you the truth, now in my eighties, I'm still looking for the right one! -RBP

Age comes on slowly, imperceptibly; you are hardly aware of it, until one day you look in the mirror and there you are, an old woman with all the accoutrements of old age.

But don't despair; there are benefits, too. A lot of people get up and give you a seat in the subway or on the bus, you get a discount on movie tickets, and many times life hands you situations that bring on laughter, even though underneath you really feel like crying.

I lost my husband in the year 1998. For two years, I was in a deep depression. I became ill; I didn't want to go anywhere or do anything. I live in Florida during the winter months. Many of my friends and neighbors there were concerned about my situation. Mostly they worried about my being alone, and they all advised me to find myself another man. I was at that time not open to any of their suggestions.

One winter, my good friend and neighbor, Miriam, came down to my house to welcome me back to Florida from New York.

"So," says Miriam after the enthusiastic greeting, "did you hear what happened to Jack Waldman?"

"Who is Jack Waldman?" I say.

"The Waldmans live on the fourth floor."

"I don't know them. So what happened to Jack Waldman?"

"His wife died," says Miriam, with a certain amount of candor. Yet I could see a smile in her eyes.

"That's too bad," I say.

"Well," says Miriam, "he is a very nice man, educated. He was a principal of a high school, and it's already four months that she's gone. I think he's ready to meet someone.

"So," I say with disdain, "do you want me to bring him a casserole?"

"No," she says, "he just bought a new car, and it's parked right near your windows. Just go over to him when he goes to his car and ask him about it. Tell him you're in the market for a new car and ask him how he feels about his. That's how you will meet him, and that's how you can get to know him."

"First of all, I don't know what he looks like. Secondly, I am not the least bit interested in cars, and third of all, I'm not ready."

"You'll never find a man with such an attitude," says Miriam disgustedly. "You'll see, some women is going to grab him up before you know it."

"Good for her," I say, while Miriam shakes her head in censure.

A few days later, I see a man shuffling to that car. To me he looks like he's one hundred years old. A few days later, Miriam again comes down to my apartment looking like the cat that swallowed the canary.

"I told you that some woman was going to get him," she says triumphantly. "I saw him dancing with a woman last night in the ballroom. She didn't look to be older than you."

"Well," I say, "I saw him the other day, and I didn't like the way he looked, and I didn't like the way he walked, and I didn't even like the way he breathed."

"Okay, okay," says Miriam, absolutely finished with me. And that was that.

Several days later, Miriam sees me walking to my car.

"Well, she says, "you'll never know what happened to Jack Waldman the other day."

"He got married," I answer.

And without hesitation, Miriam says, "No, he died." At which point we both start laughing, yet feeling very ashamed of ourselves at the same time.

"Look what you missed," she added, still laughing.

"Yes," I say rather philosophically. "We are here today and gone tomorrow. So let's go out to lunch."

The Center of Attention

After deciding that the experience below would make a good story, I sat down and made an outline of what it would contain. I decided to call it "The Center of Attention."

When I finished writing it, I read it to my cousin Dottie to get her reaction. Usually she is most supportive and enthusiastic about my tales, and her merry laughter tells me I have a winner.

This time, her face showed no outward sign of pleasure. She looked me straight in the eye and said, "Boy, you are really a storyteller. I didn't lose my eyelashes; they slipped off my eyes because I was laughing so much while dancing. I had them in my hands all the time."

"And another thing," she said. "I didn't fall on the floor; I sat down on the floor."

"Boy, oh boy," I said to myself. "After all these years, we're still there in our childhood competition!"

-RBP

My cousin Dottie is a very unique individual. She stands out in a crowd. Not only does her appearance elicit glances of admiration, but her outgoing personality, her frank and vocal comments on all things political, her fearlessness in challenging all mighty establishments calls forth nothing less than reverence by we who only hesitantly follow her lead.

My cousin Dottie is now in her middle eighties, but she still follows fashion's dictates. If hemlines go down, her skirts are long. If hemlines go up, her skirts are short. At eighty-five, she still wears mini-skirts. She never goes out without her fake eyelashes, and her hair is always bobbed in the latest mode. Her motto is that all things are in the mind, and you're only as young as you think. She has had her share of problems—eyes, ears, cancer, chemo, surgery of one kind or another—but nothing has defeated her. Her smile is aided by two prominent dimples, and her enthusiasm for life is infectious.

Dottie always was and still is a radical. Her heart and mind go out to the poor and downtrodden. Her dearest wish is to die fighting for humanity on the barricades. However, all this being said, my cousin Dottie will only shop in Bloomingdales and Saks Fifth Avenue, and she adores eating in posh restaurants.

I have always tried to follow her lead, without too much success. Where she is tall and slender, I am short and chubby. Where she never compromises, I am always ready for mutual concessions; where she is stoic, I am easily upset. But I have the one and only attribute which she envies. I can recite poetry by heart both in English and in Yiddish.

When I arrived in America at age seven, my dearest wish was to be her friend. Her family was the only relatives we had in America. And besides, my cousin Dottie was a real American girl. She couldn't even speak a word of Yiddish. But she, being older than I and already having a boyfriend, did not even give me a glance. The only time she looked at me, and then with disdain, was when I was called upon to recite a rather long poem in Yiddish called "*Der Zayde mit dem Retach*," or Grandfather and the Radish. Of course she had been forced to listen to it many times, because visitors seemed to enjoy hearing a little girl recite in Yiddish, although they themselves did not teach it to their own children.

As years passed, I am happy to report, my cousin Dottie and I became more than cousins; we became real friends. We shared many interests and developed a real appreciation for our differences as well as our similarities. One of those differences was that Dottie loved making unusual parties.

So, when her husband Seymour reached his seventy-fifth birthday, she decided she would surprise him during his birthday party. We the invited guests were also kept in the dark as to the surprise. We were all seated in her sun room, which had been converted into a rather large dining area, at long tables. It was evening, but the room was well lit. Dinner had been served, and we were all in a festive mood. Suddenly Dottie comes into the room and asks Seymour to please go out to the supermarket for more ice. They had run out of ice, and everyone was thirsty. As usual, Seymour complies.

When he leaves, all kinds of activities commence. Two of her women friends disappear along with Dottie. Their husbands begin to assemble strobe lights, which now shine on the one open area in the room. A tape deck is brought in, and Middle Eastern music begins to play. Then, as we all watch in fascination, the three women reappear, now dressed in belly dancing costumes.

All three, now in their seventies, have decided to take belly dancing lessons, and we are to have the pleasure of witnessing their premiere performance. This is to be Seymour's surprise.

On Seymour's return and as he approaches the doorway, ice bag in hand, the lights suddenly go out, the strobe lights go on, and the music begins to play. Seymour stands there transfixed as the three women begin to ambulate to the sensuous rhythms of the Middle East. We all gasp at the spectacle, and the ice starts melting in Seymour's hands.

Suddenly Dottie slips and starts to fall on the woman next to her, screaming that she had dislodged her eyelashes. This causes the woman to fall on the other women next to *her*. All three of them are now lying on the floor in the most bizarre positions with the lights on them, the music continuing to play, while the ice still melts in Seymour's hands.

You can imagine the howls and uproar that arise from us, the viewing audience. All of us laugh with great abandonment, especially me, when suddenly I feel the horrible sensation of my upper teeth leaving my mouth and bouncing on the floor in the darkened room.

Quietly I slip off my chair and start feeling around for them. They aren't there. They must have bounced under the table. Silently I creep under the table, making sure I am not touching anyone's legs. But as luck would have it, Sy, who happens to be a dentist, and who is seating next to me, feels me brush his foot.

"Hey," he says. "What's going on here?"

"Shush," I say. "It's only me, Roslyn."

"Roslyn," he says in a loud voice. "What the hell are you doing under the table?"

"Shush," I say, "Please lower your voice. I'm looking for my teeth."

"You're looking for your teeth?" he shouts at the top of his lungs.

Everyone stops laughing for a moment as the strobe light focuses on me, creeping out from under the table with my teeth in my hand. Hurriedly I shove my teeth back into my mouth without even bothering to wipe them off. The room explodes again into roars of laughter, while Sy starts to give me a lecture on dental hygiene.

My cousin Dottie, who has now gotten up from the floor, walks over to me and says in a disgusted voice, "You always did want to be the center of attention, even as a little girl. You and your goddamn 'Grandfather and the Radish,' always showing off." At which point we both start laughing hysterically.

"Thanks," I say to Dottie. "You finally noticed me!"

The Seder on the Nineteenth Floor

Of all the Seders attended by our diverse family, this one has never been forgotten. When reminded of the circumstances faced by all who attended, laughter always follows, and a warm feeling is evoked not only for the hardships overcome, but also for the feeling of pride in what the Seder meant for us.

One sometimes wonders at the miracle of obstacles.

-RBP

It was my turn to make the family Seder which had become a more crowded gathering with the passing years. However, a seder for thirty-one people in a two-bedroom apartment on the nineteenth floor with an eat-in kitchen boggles the mind.

I did not want to give up the agony and the satisfaction of making the family Seder when it fell to me. My cousin Dottie had taken her turn the year before and I claimed my family right to assume that honor this year.

I was determined to have an inspiring holiday in spite of two disappointments; one of my sons and his family would be spending the holiday in Italy, and my eighty-two-year-old mother was going to a kosher hotel in the Catskills. Living alone in her small apartment near her two daughters who did not adhere to kashrus, she found it too difficult to manage the meticulous cleaning which the Passover holiday required.

I put those unhappy thoughts in back of my mind. There remained the nagging problem of seating thirty-one people and still serving them a traditional Passover meal with all the logistics which this implied. "Think creatively," I told myself. "It's the spirit of the law that counts." But where was I going to put all those people?

I could place several tables into the living room, but I was afraid there would be no room to move amongst all the other furniture. Then it came to me: I could remove *all* the furniture from the room!

In its place I could toss pillows around the walls, creating comfortable seating on the floor. I could set out the thirty straw and wooden trays which I had purchased for another occasion. They would serve as stable holders for the abundant plates of liquid and solid food that would be forthcoming. The ceremonial plate with its symbols of the Pascal lamb, charosis, maror, greens, egg, matzah, cup of Elijah, holiday candles, and fresh flowers, always bought for the Passover, could all be placed on a low wooden table. It would be placed in the middle of the room. It would not only be lovely to look at but also quite reachable for those with long arms and some determination.

The more I thought about it the more it made sense. Hadn't our original ancestors been nomads? Hadn't they traveled around in tents and sat on the floor amidst rugs and pillows? Well, I had handsome rugs and pillows a-plenty, and what was missing could be brought in by our guests.

I timidly laid out my plan to my husband. At first he looked at me as though I had lost my wits. But I must confess that my power of persuasion is hard to resist, especially when I called attention to the injunction in the Haggadah not to sit upright, but recline. My husband being an engineer immediately attacked the practicalities. First, he measured me then he went around the room to mark off how many people could fit against the walls. He came to the conclusion that we were short just room for one. "Great," I said "We'll just have to squeeze in a little. "Now," said he, "let's see how many people accept your hair-brained idea."

I called my cousin Dottie first as she is the matriarch of our tribe, being the oldest of our family. To my surprise and pleasure her response to this innovative sitting arrangement was greeted with enthusiasm and laughter. Then I called the rest of our family. Both young and old agreed that it had a chance of being an extraordinary event. (As it happened they had no idea how extraordinary it would turn out to be.)

I now concentrated on the meal itself and the time needed to prepare it. I was still an energetic woman in her fifties who had a demanding career as a designer in the garment industry and was attending evening courses at New York University to finish my Masters Degree. My only available time was the week-end and so

I spent those two days and nights preparing the food for the Seder which would take place that coming Wednesday evening.

The menu was traditional: gefilte fish, soup with matzo balls (we call them *knaidlach*), highly spiced broiled chicken served with mashed potato balls and my special *tzimmes* made Moroccan style with sweet and pungent little meat balls. This is a dish of dried fruits mostly prunes, potatoes sweet and plain, with onions, garlic, salt, pepper and a dash of cinnamon, topped off with a can of pineapple cubes and its juice. Dessert was Passover cake, nuts, fruit and candy, served with tea. My brother would contribute the wine. My sister would provide the greens and charoses, the sweet paste made from apples and cinnamon to resemble the mortar our ancestors used when they were slaves. My cousins would bring the more delicious Passover deserts, and the flowers. My husband had done all the shopping for the ingredients and demanded a taste of each emerging sizzling dish which he judged as "perfection."

All was set and ready. I had only the last minute details to worry about, but these had to be done just before the start of the Seder. This had been my particular chore for the past 28 years. At every Seder made by members of our family I had prepared individual little plates of symbolic food needed for the ritual ceremony. This eliminated the turmoil of passing each necessary food item.

Twenty-eight years ago I had taken on a project of compiling a new more modern Haggadah in English, which would reflect our family's diverse Jewish identification. Many of us had gone to a Yiddish Cultural Folk school and we knew a great many charming Yiddish Passover songs. The Haggadah was a hit and we have used it ever since.

Way back in 1954, we felt the need to include the remembrance of the Holocaust, and the Warsaw Ghetto uprising which took place on Passover Eve. Six candles were lit for the six million Jews who perished during those horrific times, included among them were our large and loving families of Eastern Europe. The Haggadah was designed for total participation by all who attended. There were always guests both Jewish and Gentile invited to the Seder by various members of our family. All were proud to share this joyous occasion with strangers. The Haggadah stressed the fight for freedom, not only for Jews but for all of mankind, and the young people related to its universalism.

I planned not to go to work on Wednesday, the day of the Seder, and I looked forward to relishing the holiday spirit without the usual rush.

And then it came: The Great Spring Blizzard of 1982.

I trudged to work Tuesday through snow and wind. I was lucky the buses and subways were running. I worked through the morning in anticipation, waiting for the radio weather report to announce that the storm was abating. A call came from the main office at 11:00 AM that we were to close at 2:30, as the storm was gathering momentum and getting home would be a problem.

Hurriedly I sewed up several extra pillow casings of beautiful red satin quilted material which I had used for making robes and which still lay about in my design studio. I could not expect people to drag their own pillows through the snow. Feeling grateful for the extra time I would have because of the early closing, I packed up my bulky belongings, caught a subway and headed home. Miracles of miracles, the bus was waiting at the subway exit to take me home.

When I entered the lobby of my twenty storied apartment house I found it dark and full of agitated people. The power was out and the elevators were not running. The storm had blown out the transformers and nothing was working. Repair service was investigating.

A power failure is generally a traumatic occurrence but to have a power failure the day before Passover eve is a major catastrophe. All week the halls of this large apartment house had been full of richly pungent odors. Gefilte fish in the lobby—the spicy, tingling aroma of pot roast hung heavily in the elevators—the sweet smell of stewed fruit wafted throughout the upper floors. One could have a veritable feast of smells alone. All these gastronomical delights which were resting in stuffed refrigerators were ready to be heated and eaten on the night of the Seder. Many people had been invited to share the Passover in these apartments. The tenants were mostly middle aged Jewish men and women with grown children and grandchildren. What a calamity; warm refrigerators, snowed-in guests!

I tried not to think of the horrible possibilities. I climbed the dark staircase to the nineteenth floor with my large, cumbersome package of quilted bolster cases. I was helped by enterprising youngsters with lighted candles who, for a small tip and a large sense of usefulness, helped weary home-comers to their respective apartments.

When I came into the kitchen I found a note from my husband telling me that he was at home when the power failure occurred. He had sanitized the bath tub and filled it with water. His note stressed that I use water sparingly as the pumps which supply the water power were out. There would be no water in either the kitchen or bathroom until the power was restored. He had gone to do the last minute shopping before the storm closed the stores. Don't panic, I told myself, it's all going to be repaired, if not today, then surely tomorrow morning.

But try as I might, the prospect of having no light, no heat, no water, no toilet facilities, no electricity of any kind, filled me with dread. We were virtual prisoners on the nineteenth floor.

My husband returned out of breath from his arduous climb, but he did not waste a minute before telling me that we must immediately start gathering as many candles as we could find. Darkness was fast approaching and we had to be ready for any emergency. Outside the storm raged with renewed fury, inside we went about wrapped in gloom and cold. The windows were frosted with wintry designs as we ate our cold supper in the glow of candlelight. We went to bed early. With two comforters piled high, one on the other, we lay close to each other in the dark, closer than usual.

The storm had abated overnight. Before my husband left for work the next morning, he assured me that he would not have to walk up the stairs on coming home. He is an engineer and has implicit faith in man's ability to handle machinery. I spent the morning putting the final touches to the gay pillows lining the walls, polishing the silver and rubbing the brass Elijah cup until it glowed like the sun.

I was having a snack with my neighbor when the telephone started ringing, the first of many calls to inquire about our power failure. They had heard about our community's disaster on the radio and the whole family was alerted. I assured them that all would be well.

At 4:30 p.m., the power was still out. I called my cousin Dottie to discuss the seriousness of the situation. I could not expect thirty people to walk up nineteen flights of stairs, even though there were now many *yahrtzeit* candles lighting the way on all floors. There were babies and older people involved who I felt could not possibly make it. And then there was the problem of heating the food in electric ovens that didn't work.

My cousin's son answered the phone. He had come from Madison, Wisconsin, with his wife and thirteen-month-old little girl, Sara. He was looking forward to getting together with all his cousins at the Seder, he said. I told him my tale of woe, stressing the impossibility of overcoming so many impediments. His reply was unexpected, exhilarating, even though I realized its loving foolhardiness.

"My dear cousin, once removed," he said, "Had not our ancestors traveled around in tents in the desert for forty years in the heat and cold? Did they not do without the aid of electric lights, hot and cold running water, steam heat, toilet facilities, micro-ovens and automatic elevators? Are we less Jews than they were? Do you think we have been so spoiled and cuddled by our secular, industrial, materialistic bourgeois society that we can't walk up nineteen flights of stairs carrying children, blankets, tons of fruit, nuts, and assorted cakes, to say nothing of candles, flashlights, and pillows?" I told him to forget the pillows. "Great," he said. However they would only come if I could find a way of warming up my delicious food, no *knaidlach*—no Seder. I assured him that I could by using my neighbor's gas oven, but there would be one more person at the Seder, my neighbor.

And so it came to pass; one family member called the other, each one becoming more excited at the prospect of the challenge to their spirit of adventure, their pleasure of sharing with one another a real test of endurance against a whim of nature, a gathering of the clan under stress and hardship.

My son and grandchildren from Syracuse found it a thrill and delight. Never had they experienced so much fun. My youngest son and his bride came puffing up the stairs with eyes shining. My sister, nephew and assorted friends stumbled in singing and laughing. My cousin's children and grandchildren arrived loaded down with their gear and provisions amidst shouts of approval and admiration.

My neighbor joined the excited gathering.

Only my brother, his wife, sons, and mother-in-law did not make it up the stairs. He has a nerve condition which incapacitates him and limits his movements. Though he knew the power was out, he came anyway hoping against hope the electricity would be restored in time. It was not. After waiting a considerable time in the lobby, he sent one of his sons up the nineteen flights of stairs to bring his promised wine. All cried out in sympathy and disappointment as a beloved nephew and cousin went back down those dark and formidable stairs—but not before stuffing his mouth full of all the favorite Passover goodies he could find.

The house was cold, the glowing candlelight softened shapes and faces. Mystery, awe and wonder enveloped us all as we sat on the rugs against the many pillows wrapped in shawls and blankets. We started reading the Haggadah and when we came to the *"Ma nishtano ha-lilo hazeh,"* "Why is this night different than any other night?" we all laughed hysterically.

It was a most beautiful and soul-searching Seder. Questions were asked and issues discussed. The time-honored Seder service which belonged to this family only was recited and sung with greater love and commitment than ever before. And when the door was opened into the darkened hallway for Elijah to come in and sip from his cup of wine to the beautiful sounds of the song "Eliyahu Ha–Nuvi," we all knew a miracle had really happened.

Going Home to Nowhere

When I originally wrote this story, it was much longer than it finally became. It hurts me too much to tell the whole thing. -*RBP*

In the summer of 1991, when I was sixty-nine years old, I went back to my shtetl, my small town of Wysokie Litewsk, in what is now Belarus. It was something I had looked forward to since, as a child of seven, I arrived in America with my mother in 1929. I arranged for a man named Shlomo Gavrilivetz Kantronovich to be my guide. When I was a child, the town had three thousand people, almost all of them Jews. He was now the only Jew left in the entire area.

We parked the car and started to walk around the green. When I asked Shlomo where this unpaved little street led, he answered, to the *lunke*, the meadow.

"This is my street!" I said. "My house was a little way down the road."

I started to walk very fast, and there it stood, right where I knew it would be. It looked different now, with its painted window boxes and new fence, but there was no mistaking it; this was my house. I walked around to the back, and, sure enough, there in the corner of the house, behind the kitchen and the bedroom, stood the old crab apple tree I had watched go into bloom so many springs before.

I did not want to go into my house. I couldn't bear it. I walked further down the road to my grandparents' house, right across from the old synagogue. Nothing is there except tall weeds.

"You see this old *shul*?" said Shlomo. "It's the only shul left standing in the shtetl. The Germans used it as a jail. See the bars on the windows?"

I looked closely. There among the decaying wooden frames, I see the bars. We walked a little further, past my Aunt Golde's house, which is no longer there. And then I see it: the new synagogue. The one built just before we left for America. I remember how proud everyone was of it. It was so grand and elegant, with its stained glass windows and wonderful candelabra. It had two awesome golden lions carved alongside the altar, where the Toyre was kept. Guardians of the Faith.

I stand and look at its destroyed walls; trees are growing out of its center, surrounded by pieces of wall that refused to give way. I can't take it anymore. I can't seem to swallow the lump in my throat. My knees want to buckle.

I sit down on a stone, my head swimming. And then I see them: my family, my whole family, dressed in their holiday clothes for Rosh Hoshana, the Jewish New Year. So proud, going to the new synagogue to pray, and to hear my young uncle, Avrom Layb, blow the shofar, ram's horn, for the very first time in that new holy place.

I sit on that stone for a long time, just staring, as they walk past me into the ruins. Much later, after I finally stop crying, I see the meadow, the woods, the sky, the stork nests and the sunflowers. I have not spoken to a single person in my little town. I could not find a single gravestone in what had been the Jewish cemetery. It is now a government housing project. I had come and gone without finding out anything. The records of the Jews I was told by the city clerk had been sent to Kiev, where they were said to have been destroyed in a fire.

I couldn't wait to leave this tragic place that had once been my whole world.

Glossary of Yiddish Terms

When Roslyn tells her stories to audiences that may be unfamiliar with Yiddish terms, she weaves the explanations into her tale. So as not to break the flow of some of the printed stories, however, we've included some brief definitions here. One of the best, and certainly the liveliest, source for Yiddish terms is still the classic The Joys of Yiddish, *by Leo Rosten (New York: McGraw Hill, 1968), from which many of these definitions were adapted.* *-CSN*

Challah: A traditional Jewish egg bread eaten on the Sabbath and on all Jewish holidays except Passover, when leavened bread is forbidden.

Chuppa: Wedding canopy.

Chutzpah: Gall, brazen nerve, presumption combined with arrogance.

Dreidel: Top-like toy played with on Hanukkah.

Fier kashas: Literally, "the four questions," read by the youngest child at the Seder from the Passover Haggada. The answers tell the story of the holiday.

Goyim: Gentiles

Haggada: The narrative read at the Seder, which includes Rabbinic comments, hymns, prayers, questions and answers.

Kiddush: Ceremonial blessing over wine for Sabbath and holidays.

Kreplach: Jewish dumplings

Latkes: Potato pancakes, a traditional food for Hanukkah.

L'chaim: A toast over wine or other alcoholic drinks, meaning "To Life!"

Mensch: A human being, an upright, honorable, decent person, someone of consequence, someone to admire, a noble person

Passover (Pesakh): The most cherished Jewish holiday, the festival of freedom, lasting eight days, and commemorating Israel's dramatic deliverance from enslavement in Egypt more than 2,000 years ago, as recounted in the Old Testament book of Exodus.

Purim: The Feast of Lots, commemorating the rescue of the Jews of Persia from Haman's plot to exterminate them. The story is found in the Book of Esther, in the Old Testament.

Pushke: A little can or container kept in the home, often in the kitchen, in which money is accumulated to be donated to charity.

Seder: The celebratory meal of Passover where the recounting of the Exodus from Egypt takes place.

Shabbes: The Jewish Sabbath, beginning Friday at sundown and ending Saturday night

Shekhinah: The term used to symbolize God's dazzling, shining spirit and presence. The Shekhinah often related to as the feminine aspect of God.

Shmatte: Rag

Shpiel: Play

Treyf: Not kosher

Yahrzeit: Memorial day for the dead

About the Author

Roslyn Bresnick-Perry was born in Wysokie Litewskie, in what is now Belarus. She emigrated to New York City in 1929, at the age of seven. Her wisdom and humor have captivated audiences at storytelling festivals theaters throughout the country and abroad, including the prestigious National Storytelling Festival in Tennessee, the Smithsonian Folklife Festival, the Victory Theater on Broadway and the Library of Congress, and she has served as teller-in-residence at the International Storytelling Center. Her work has also been broadcast on National Public Radio.

A retired fashion designer, Ms. Perry holds a Master of Arts degree in Cultural History from New York University and received her Bachelor of Arts from Fordham University. She conducts workshops and seminars at institutions including Queens College, New York and Syracuse universities, and the University of Arizona. She has published *Leaving for America*, a children's book, and book of poetry, her recordings have won American Library Association awards, and her stories and translations are featured in several collections. Winner of the prestigious Lifetime Achievement Award from the National Storytelling Network, Ms. Perry now divides her time between New York and Deerfield Beach, Florida.

About the Editor

Caren Schnur Neile, MFA, Ph.D., directs the South Florida Storytelling Project at Florida Atlantic University, where she is artist-in-residence in the School of Communication and Multimedia Studies. Dr. Neile performs and presents workshops and lectures across the U.S. and overseas, particularly on the topics of storytelling for social justice and with the elderly. A Fulbright Senior Specialist, she is a founding editor of *Storytelling, Self, Society: An Interdisciplinary Journal of Storytelling Studies* (Taylor & Francis) and founder of the Palm Beach County Storytelling Guild. Her publications include *Hidden: A Sister and Brother in Nazi Poland* (co-author, University of Wissonsin Press), numerous magazine and journal articles and several chapters in collections.

Dr. Neile is a board member of the National Storytelling Network and a former board member of the Florida Storytelling Association and the Healing Story Alliance. Among her other grants and awards, she is also a recipient of an Oracle award for Regional Service and Leadership from the National Storytelling Network. She lives in Boca Raton, Florida.

LISTEN ONLINE
to Roslyn Bresnick-Perry

Visit http://www.benyehudapress.com/go/rbp to hear Roslyn Bresnick-Perry, author of I Loved My Mother on Saturdays, tell her story "My Sister on the Hood." She's as funny and engaging talking about New York City as she is about her shtetl childhood. If you haven't had the pleasure of hearing Roslyn Bresnick-Perry live, you're in for a treat!

If you love this book, LET THE WORLD KNOW!

If you enjoyed this book, and are glad you read it, share the love! Consider writing a brief review on Amazon.com or BN.com or LibraryThing.com, sharing a note on Facebook, or even writing us at editors@BenYehudaPress.com. Go ahead: Make the author's day!

CONNECT WITH *Ben Yehuda Press*

Visit http://www.BenYehudaPress.com or look us up on Facebook to find out about new titles and special offers.

Show your support for independent Jewish publishing by joining our mailing list or friending us on Facebook.

Our titles span the diversity of the Jewish experience.

We depend on readers like you who care about great books, well-told stories and ideas old and new.

MEET THE BOLD WOMEN
of our exciting fiction

The Cabalist's Daughter: A Novel of Practical Messianic Redemption

Yori Yanover

The master mystic is cloned—and his messianic offspring is a girl! Magic, mayhem and social commentary abound in this comic, cosmic, irreverent Kabbalistic thriller. ***"A wildly-fun, Jewish Hitchhiker's Guide to the Galaxy,"*** says Laurie Gwen Shapiro, author of The Matzo Ball Heiress.

A Delightful Compendium of Consolation: A Fabulous Tale of Romance, Adventure and Faith in the Medieval Mediterranean

Burton L. Visotzky.

What's a nice Jewish girl doing as a desert brigand? Find out in this historical novel of the 11th century where the Arabian Nights meets the tales of the Talmud. ***"I couldn't put it down,"*** says Maggie Anton, author of Rashi's Daughters.

Bessie: A Novel of Love and Revolution

Lawrence Bush

The story of a girl who ran off to join the revolution, from her shetl childhood through her Russian hardships to a life in America as activist, mother, and Yiddish-accented bubbe. ***"A marvelous story about an amazing woman. It will grip you from beginning to end,"*** says Hadassah Magazine.

The Lilac Tree

Nicolette Maleckar

The war is over. But Hanne Goldshmidt's adventures in Berlin, 1945, are only beginning. An incandescent story of the first blush of love in an impossible time, filled with an indomitable s pirit of hope and joy. ***"I'm struck by the humor and the fairy-tale quality of the characters,"*** says Allegheny Mountain Radio.

DISCOVER DEEP SPIRITUALITY
in the Jewish tradition

Torah Journeys: The Inner Path to the Promised Land

Rabbi Shefa Gold

The weekly Torah portion becomes a path of spiritual growth and personal development in this important work of Jewish renewal. ***"A remarkable book of profound depth. It has taught me much,"*** says Archbishop Emeritus Desmond Tutu. ***"One of the best Jewish books of 2006,"*** says Beliefnet.com.

In the Fever of Love: An Illumination of the Song of Songs

Rabbi Shefa Gold

A leading rabbi looks to the Bible's sexiest book to spice up your romances with God and your Beloved. This poetic response to the Song of Songs moves from the Biblical verses to a deeply personal, highly erotic meditation on the love of God. ***"Readers of*** IN THE FEVER OF LOVE ***will be inspired and led deeper into their own souls by its shimmering interpretations,"*** says Alicia Ostriker, author of For the Love of God: The Bible as an Open Book.

Torah and Company

Judith Z. Abrams

Discover the fun of Talmudic debate with this guide to interactive Torah study designed to spice up your family's Sabbath table. ***"Reveals the power and relevance of each weekly Torah portion. A Shabbat treasure for every home,"*** says Rabbi Goldie Milgram, author of Reclaiming Judaism as a Spiritual Practice.

FIND LAUGHTER AND TEARS
in our moving memoirs

The Wicked Wit of the West: The Last Great Golden Age Screenwriter Shares the Hilarity and Heartaches of Working With Groucho, Garland, Gleason, Burns, Berle, Benny, and many more

Irving Brecher as told to Hank Rosenfeld

The story of "the funniest man you never heard of" and how his wicked wit took him from Vaudeville to YouTube. ***"Brimming with delectable anecdotes,"*** says the Boston Herald. ***"Altogether delightful, this is an incredible reminiscence by a remarkable man,"*** says Library Journal.

Life in the Present Tense: Reflections on Family and Faith

Rifka Rosenwein

With equal parts humor and heartache—the heartache supplied after the author's cancer diagnosis—Rosenswein deals with aging parents, challenging modern schedules, timeless holy days and the joys of raising her three children. ***"A treasure trove of wisdom from one of American Judaism's most beloved and lamented voices,"*** says Publisher's Weekly.

Waiting for God: The Spiritual Reflections of a Reluctant Atheist

Lawrence Bush

The most Jewish atheist you'll ever meet is a thoughtful tour guide through the worlds of baby boomer spirituality. *"He writes about non-belief with an empathy for believers missing from the works of the New Atheists,"* says the New Jersey Jewish News.

Printed in the United States
214793BV00006B/1/P

9 781934 730300